EGG & CHICKEN WITH CHEF GRANT MACPHERSON - PHOTOGRAPHY BY BILL MILNE

THIS EDITION FIRST PUBLISHED BY 1010 PRINTING IN CHINA
PUBLISHER - SCOTCH MYST INC

ISBN 978-1-7923-7960-4

BOOK PUBLISHING TEAM
DESIGN CONCEPT AND COVER – BILL MILNE
PHOTOGRAPHER – BILL MILNE

LOGISTICS , ASSISTANT PHOTOGRAPHER – MOJAHED REAZ
PRODUCTION ASSISTANT-NOAH ROSENBAUM
WRITER/EDITOR – LIZ CRAIN
BOOK ADVISOR – RHONDA HUGHES
BOOK COLLABORATOR – CINDY LASAR

CULINARY TEAM
CHEF – GRANT MACPHERSON
CULINARY DEVELOPMENT – ALEJANDRO SANDOVAL
SOUS CHEF - ALL-AROUND GREAT GUY – CHEF SAMUEL MORSE

SPECIAL THANKS TO
AMERICAN EGG BOARD
STEELITE – CHINA AND SILVERWARE
MATFER BOURGEAT– CULINARY TOOLS, KITCHEN UTENSILS
WEST COAST PRIME
CHEF JEAN-GEORGES VONGERICHTEN

IMPORTANT: THOSE INDIVIDUALS WHO MIGHT BE AT RISK OF CERTAIN FOOD ALLERGIES, THE ELDERLY,
PREGNANT WOMEN, SMALL CHILDREN AND THOSE SUFFERING FROM IMMUNE DEFICIENCIES SHOULD
CONSULT THEIR PHYSICIAN FOR ANY CONCERNS WITH INGREDIENTS IN ANY OF THE RECIPES.

GRANT

For the past decade-plus cooking for me has been one part passion, craft, and creativity, as well as one part health consciousness. All of that goes hand-in-hand in this cookbook because, well, you only get one life. Let's make it as fun and fulfilling as possible **AND** make it last by eating good-for-you food. Delicious and nutritious.

Eggs and chicken are two very tasty, readily available to most, proteins that I've adored all of my life - while growing up in Canada , while working and opening hotel restaurants throughout Asia and beyond, and while cooking at home for my boys. They're both good eaters and they really appreciate my cooking, thank goodness!

I've worked with my dear friend Bill Milne, this book's esteemed photographer, for nearly 20 years on all sorts of cooking and cookbook projects all over the world. Spin a globe with your eyes shut, put your finger down on it, and we've probably been there and worked there, wherever it is. Egg & Chicken simply stemmed from our desire to work on another book together. To get the cookbook band back together, as they say.

I really hope that you have fun with these recipes and stories that travel from Scotland to Singapore, from India to Italy. I worked hard to make sure that both the recipe steps and ingredients for all of the dishes aren't too tricky to do or hard to obtain. That's because I want you to enjoy yourself. We had a lot of fun putting this book and its stories together. So, I really hope that you have fun too when cooking these recipes at home for you and your loved ones.

BILL

I've had the great pleasure of working with my dear and ultra-talented friend, Grant, on all sorts of projects since 2004, when we teamed up to open Wynn Las Vegas. Grant was in charge of all of the hotel's food and drink, and building the menus and dining culture at all of its restaurants. I was in charge of photographing everything. I lived in that hotel for the better part of the year doing that, and Grant and I became lifelong friends and collaborators during that time.

Since then, we've travelled to work together everywhere from France, Italy, Australia, and Canada, to throughout Asia, and then some, on all sorts of cool, sometimes pretty rock & roll, food and drink projects. Grant and I love each other like family after all these years of collaborating. I'm guessing that you'll pick up on that throughout *Egg & Chicken*.

Of course, when you work and travel with someone so frequently, you dine with them. Grant and I both have a deep and abiding love for breakfast and brunch, and soft and custardy scrambled eggs (see page 18e) are one of our all-time favorites. Any time of day. We also eat a lot of chicken dishes while working together too. One of my very favorite recipes in this book is Grant's Scottish Chicken Pie (see page 44c). It turns out that you aren't as lucky as me, because you most likely won't get Grant to whip that up for you, but you can now easily make it at home. And I highly recommend that you do. Ok, get cooking!

Bill

Working Remote on the Egg and Chicken book

- Grant and Bill

I'VE KNOWN GRANT FOR OVER 25 YEARS SINCE WE OPENED PRIME AT THE BELLAGIO HOTEL IN LAS VEGAS TOGETHER.
HIS DEDICATION TO EXCELLENCE IN ORGANIZATION AND OPERATIONS AS WELL AS HIS CULINARY KNOWLEDGE HAS MADE HIM A WORLD CLASS CHEF.
IT WAS A GREAT PLEASURE AND HONOR WHEN HE ASKED ME TO BE PART OF HIS NEW BOOK EGG+CHICKEN.
THANK YOU, MY FRIEND.

JEAN-GEORGES VONGERICHTEN

Jean-Georges Vongerichten - Nyc

EGG
AM

EGGSAM

Soft-Boiled Egg Cups & Buttery Soldiers
Egg & BLT Tacos
Street-Style Cheesy Egg & Bacon Bagel
Corned Beef Hash & Poached Eggs
Hard-Boiled Eggs & Lemony Herb Salad
Scrambled Eggs, Shaved Asparagus Salad & Toasted Baguette
Egg White & Avocado Omelet
Devilish Eggs
Vegetable-Loaded Frittata & Osetra Caviar
Avocado Toast & Poached Eggs
Over-Easy Eggs & Cantaloupe
Blueberry Pancakes & Compote
Eggs Benny
Egg Drop Soup
Egg Fried Rice
Seasonal Berries & Champagne Sabayon

Soft-Boiled Egg Cups & Buttery Soldiers

MAKES 4 SERVINGS

SOFT-BOILED EGGS ARE MY FAVORITE, WHEN IT COMES TO BOILED EGGS, AND THIS IS SUCH A LOVELY, QUICK, AND EASY BREAKFAST. IN SCOTLAND GROWING UP, EGG CUPS WERE A COMMON BREAKFAST AT HOME. I'D SEASON MINE A BIT WITH SALT AND PEPPER, AND ENJOY THEM WITH A SPOON RIGHT OUT OF THE SHELL, ALONG WITH SOME NICE BUTTERED TOAST. SO GOOD.

ALTHOUGH AN EGG TOPPER IS FAIRLY EASY TO PURCHASE THESE DAYS ONLINE OR OTHERWISE, AS ARE EGG CUPS, YOU CERTAINLY DON'T NEED EITHER TO MAKE THIS RECIPE. IF YOU DON'T HAVE EGG CUPS YOU CAN GO AHEAD AND USE SHOT GLASSES. AND, IF YOU MAKE THESE WITHOUT AN EGG TOPPER, EITHER SIMPLY BUT GENTLY PEEL THE EGGS, AND THEN SLICE THEM IN HALF ON THE PLATE, SO THAT YOU DON'T LOSE ANY OF THE DELICIOUS YOLK. OR, YOU COULD JUST USE A SPOON TO TAP AND CRACK THEM OPEN IN THE CUP. I RECOMMEND GETTING AN EGG TOPPER THOUGH. YOU'LL FEEL LIKE A RESTAURANT CHEF IN YOUR OWN HOME.

---

4 LARGE EGGS
4 SLICES WHOLE WHEAT BREAD
4 TABLESPOONS UNSALTED BUTTER
KOSHER SALT AND FRESHLY GROUND BLACK PEPPER

OVER HIGH HEAT, BRING A MEDIUM POT OF WATER TO A BOIL. ONCE BOILING, GENTLY ADD THE EGGS TO THE WATER AND MAINTAIN A SIMMER FOR 8 MINUTES. USE A SLOTTED SPOON TO REMOVE THE EGGS FROM THE WATER. PAT THEM DRY AND PLACE EACH IN AN EGG CUP. USE AN EGG TOPPER TO REMOVE THE TOP OF EACH SHELL. SEASON WITH SALT AND PEPPER.

TOAST THE BREAD TO YOUR LIKING. WHILE STILL HOT, BUTTER EACH SLICE WITH ABOUT 1 TABLESPOON OF BUTTER. TRIM THE CRUST OFF THE TOAST AND EVENLY CUT EACH SLICE INTO 3 PIECES. SERVE THE EGG CUPS ON PLATES WITH THE BUTTERED SOLDIERS.

Egg & BLT Tacos

Makes 4 to 6 servings, 12 tacos

I played around with this recipe for a while before I got it right. I really wanted a breakfast and brunch taco that would show off eggs in a tasty way, but also be really beautiful and colorful. These tacos do all of that and, lucky for you, they are quick and easy to put together.

---

12 slices thick-cut applewood-smoked bacon
1 cup mayonnaise
1 teaspoon Greek yogurt
1 teaspoon chopped fresh chives
Juice of 1/2 lemon
Kosher salt and freshly ground black pepper
4 large eggs
12 small (6-inch) soft flour tortillas
1 cup thinly sliced iceberg lettuce
2 medium tomatoes, diced
1 cup shaved Parmesan, for garnish
Lemon Oil (see page 60c), for Finishing

Preheat the oven to 350 degrees F.

Line a rimmed baking sheet with parchment paper, arrange the bacon strips on it in a single layer without overlapping, and bake for 12 to 15 minutes, or until golden brown. Set aside. Chop the bacon into 2-inch pieces, and save and chop the trimmings (about 1/4 cup) for the aioli.

In a small bowl, mix together the mayonnaise, yogurt, chives, lemon juice, and the bacon trimmings. Season with salt and pepper.

Over high heat, bring a medium pot of water to a boil. Once boiling, gently add the eggs to the water and maintain a simmer for 9 to 10 minutes. Use a slotted spoon to transfer the eggs into an ice water-bath to cool. Once cooled, peel the eggs under cold running water then pat dry. Slice them crosswise evenly into thirds.

In a medium nonstick pan over high heat, toast the tortillas on each side for 5 to 10 seconds until warmed. Spread 1 teaspoon of bacon aioli onto each warmed tortilla. Add about 2 tablespoons of lettuce, and 2 tablespoons of tomatoes, to each tortilla along with a piece of bacon, a slice of egg, and a Parmesan cheese shaving. Serve the remaining aioli in a small dish on the side. Season the eggs with salt, and pepper, and drizzle with the lemon oil.

Street-Style Cheesy Egg & Bacon Bagel

MAKES 4 SERVINGS

When I moved to the U.S. in 1998, I had my first bagel, and for a while, really through all of my years cooking at the Bellagio in Las Vegas, I didn't really care for them. As I get older, I like them more and more. Now I think a good fresh bagel that's toasted and buttered is fantastic. And, every now and again a bagel sandwich like this really hits the spot. As far as bacon goes, I like mine crispy and not swimming in grease.

---

8 SLICES THICK-CUT APPLEWOOD SMOKED BACON
4 LARGE EGGS
1 TABLESPOON UNSALTED BUTTER
4 PLAIN BAGELS, HALVED
1/4 CUP MAYONNAISE
1 CUP LOOSELY PACKED STEMMED ARUGULA
4 THICK SLICED PIECES OF VERMONT CHEDDAR CHEESE

Preheat the oven to 350 degrees F.

Line a rimmed baking sheet lined with parchment paper, arrange the bacon strips on it in a single layer without overlapping, and bake for 12 to 15 minutes, or until golden brown. Set aside.

Cook the eggs over easy in butter in ring molds the same size as the bagels.

NOTE: If you don't have ring molds you can simply use your spatula to form the eggs roughly into the shape of the bagels.

Toast the bagels until golden brown.
Lightly spread all toasted bagel halves equally with mayonnaise. Top half of them with 1/4 cup of arugula, 2 strips of bacon, 1 slice of cheddar, and top with a cooked egg. Complete each bagel sandwich by topping it with a second bagel half. Lightly press down on it, and wrap the sandwich in aluminum foil.

Corned Beef Hash & Poached Eggs

MAKES 4 SERVINGS

Growing up in Dundee, Scotland my mother made corned beef hash for us a lot. At its heart, it's a leftovers dish. You have corned beef supper on Saturday, let's say, and the leftovers become corned beef hash breakfast or lunch that Sunday. I honestly didn't really like it growing up. It was just something we had to eat. Now, I love it. The runny poached eggs here along with all the crispy bits of corned beef plus the sweet potatoes are so good. I've been making corned beef and refining it for about 30 years now. So, I've passed that knowledge gained to you here. Beware, this is a filling hash so a nap might be in order after.

BUERRE BLANC

1 TABLESPOON PLUS 1 TEASPOON GRAPESEED OIL (OR OTHER NEUTRAL OIL), DIVIDED
1 SHALLOT, SLICED, PLUS 1 TABLESPOON FINELY DICED SHALLOT, DIVIDED
2 TABLESPOONS WHITE WINE VINEGAR
1/4 CUP WHITE WINE
3 SPRIGS FRESH THYME
1 BAY LEAF
1 TABLESPOON HEAVY CREAM
4 TABLESPOONS (1/2 STICK) UNSALTED BUTTER, CUT INTO 6 PIECES
KOSHER SALT AND FRESHLY GROUND BLACK PEPPER

HASH

2 CUPS PEELED AND DICED SWEET POTATOES
2 CUPS DICED CORNED BEEF
1/4 CUP PEELED AND JULIENNED RIPE TOMATOES
1 TEASPOON CHOPPED FRESH CURLY-LEAF PARSLEY
KOSHER SALT AND FRESHLY GROUND BLACK PEPPER
2 TABLESPOONS DISTILLED WHITE VINEGAR
4 LARGE EGGS

In a small pot over medium heat, warm 1 teaspoon of the oil. Add the entire sliced shallot and cook, stirring occasionally, for about 2 minutes, or until soft. Add the white wine vinegar, along with the white wine, thyme, and bay leaf, and bring to a boil. Lower the heat and simmer for about 2 minutes, until it's reduced by about half.

Strain the sauce through a fine-mesh sieve, discarding the thyme and bay leaf, into a medium pot over medium heat. While rapidly whisking, add the cream then slowly add the butter pieces, one at a time. Whisk until the beurre blanc thickens to the consistency of hollandaise. Season to taste with salt and pepper.

In a medium nonstick pan over medium-high heat, heat the remaining tablespoon of oil. Once hot, add the remaining 1 tablespoon of finely diced shallot, and sweet potatoes, and cook for 4 to 5 minutes, moving them in the pan very little, until the potatoes have browned. Add the corned beef, tomatoes, and parsley, and cook for 2 to 3 more minutes. Season to taste with salt and pepper.

Over high heat, bring a medium pot of water to a boil. Meanwhile, pour the distilled white vinegar into a medium bowl and gently crack the eggs into the bowl. Once the water comes to a boil, lower the heat to maintain a simmer. Use a slotted spoon to carefully slide one egg at a time into the water. Poach until the whites are set but the yolks are still runny, about 4 minutes. Use a slotted spoon to transfer the eggs to a bowl.

Place a 3-inch ring mold in the center of a wide single serving bowl and lightly press 1 cup of the corned beef hash into the mold. Place 1 poached egg on top of the hash then carefully remove the ring mold. Spoon 1 to 2 tablespoons of beurre blanc over and around the egg and hash. Repeat with the remaining eggs and hash.

Hard-Boiled Eggs & Lemony Herb Salad

MAKES 2 TO 4 SERVINGS

ONE OF MY FAVORITE THINGS ABOUT THIS TASTY BREAKFAST IS THE LEMON OIL (SEE PAGE 60C). ACID IS AN EXCELLENT DIGESTIVE AID, AND WE ALL CAN USE A LITTLE HELP WITH THAT IN THE MORNING. FRESHLY SQUEEZED LEMON JUICE, PLUS LEMON ZEST AND OIL, IS IN A LOT OF MY RECIPES FOR THAT REASON. I ALSO LOVE THE BRIGHTNESS AND BIT OF SPARKLE THAT LEMON ALWAYS ADDS. I PROMISE YOU'LL GET SOME WELL-DESERVED PEP IN YOUR STEP FROM THIS FRESH, HERBY BREAKFAST.

---

4 LARGE EGGS
2 TABLESPOONS CHOPPED FRESH TARRAGON
2 TABLESPOONS THINLY SLICED FRESH FENNEL
2 TABLESPOONS CHOPPED FRESH DILL
1/2 TEASPOON LEMON OIL (SEE PAGE 60C)
KOSHER SALT AND FRESHLY GROUND BLACK PEPPER

OVER HIGH HEAT, BRING A MEDIUM POT OF WATER TO A BOIL. ONCE BOILING, GENTLY ADD THE EGGS TO THE WATER AND MAINTAIN A SIMMER FOR 12 MINUTES.

USE A SLOTTED SPOON TO TRANSFER THE EGGS INTO AN ICE WATER-BATH TO COOL. ONCE COOLED, PEEL THE EGGS UNDER COLD RUNNING WATER THEN PAT DRY.

IN A SMALL BOWL COMBINE THE TARRAGON, FENNEL, DILL, AND LEMON OIL.

CUT THE EGGS IN HALF LENGTHWISE AND PLACE THE HALVES ON A CERAMIC EGG CARTON FOR SERVING IF YOU HAVE ONE, OR ON A PLATE OR PLATTER IF NOT. SEASON THE EGGS WITH PEPPER, AND FILL THE EMPTY SLOTS OF THE CARTON WITH THE HERB SALAD.

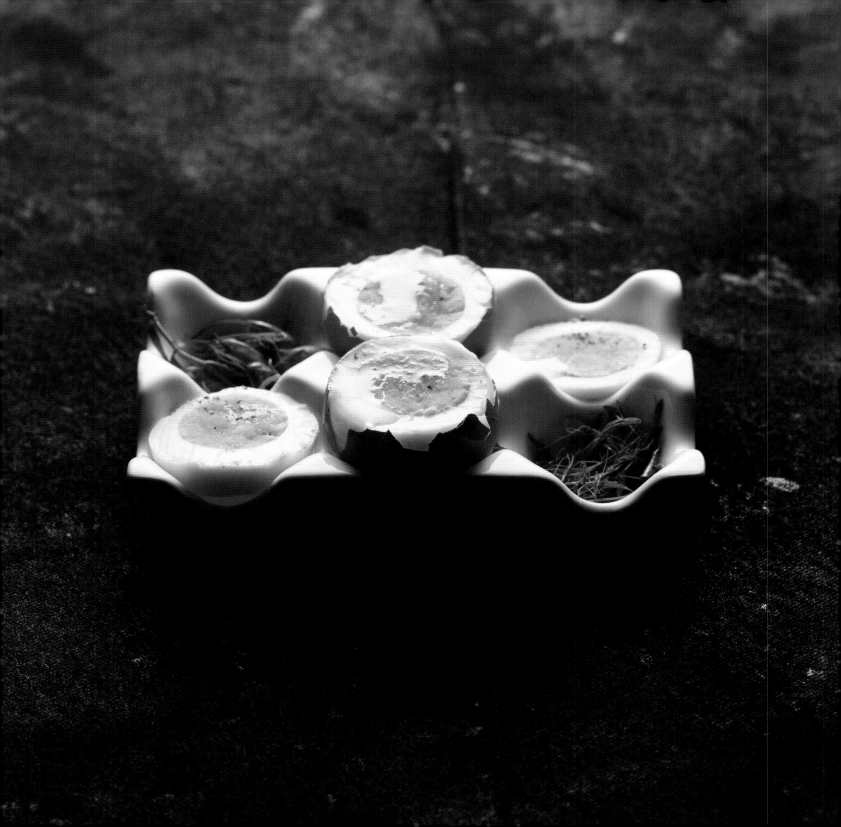

Scrambled Eggs, Shaved Asparagus Salad & Toasted Baguette

MAKES 4 SERVINGS

THE KEY TO GREAT SCRAMBLED EGGS IS TO MAKE SURE THAT THE EGGS ARE FULLY EMULSIFIED BEFORE SLIDING THEM INTO THE PAN. AND, ONCE YOU GET THEM INTO THE PAN, COOK THEM SLOWLY AND GENTLY. I RECOMMEND MAKING THIS DISH IN THE SPRING WHEN ASPARAGUS IS AT ITS PEAK AND SO BEAUTIFUL. GO FOR ASPARAGUS THAT'S MEDIUM WIDTH, AND NOT TOO THICK OR TOO THIN. PUT A LITTLE ASPARAGUS SALAD ON TOP OF YOUR TOASTED BAGUETTE, TAKE A BITE OF CUSTARDY SCRAMBLED EGG, AND OH MY GOODNESS -- SO DELICIOUS.

---

8 LARGE EGGS
KOSHER SALT AND FRESHLY GROUND BLACK PEPPER
2 TABLESPOONS UNSALTED BUTTER, DIVIDED
4 (1/4-INCH THICK) PIECES OF BAGUETTE SLICED DIAGONALLY, TOASTED AND BUTTERED
2 CUPS SHAVED ASPARAGUS, THINLY SHAVED WITH A VEGETABLE PEELER
FINELY GRATED ZEST OF 1 MEDIUM LEMON (ABOUT 2 TABLESPOONS)
2 TEASPOONS LEMON OIL (SEE PAGE 60C)
1 TEASPOON CHOPPED FRESH CHIVES, PLUS MORE FOR GARNISH

IN A LARGE BOWL, WHISK THE EGGS UNTIL FULLY COMBINED, AND SEASON WITH SALT AND PEPPER. IN A LARGE NONSTICK PAN OVER MEDIUM HEAT, ADD 1 TABLESPOON OF THE BUTTER. ONCE HOT, POUR IN HALF OF THE EGGS. WITH A SOFT HEATPROOF SPATULA, STIR SLOWLY AND REGULARLY. COOK FOR 4 TO 5 MINUTES, UNTIL THE EGGS ARE SET IN CUSTARDY CURDS BUT STILL SLIGHTLY RUNNY. TRANSFER TO A PLATE, AND SET ASIDE. COOK THE REMAINING EGGS THE SAME WAY.

NOTE: **IF YOU STIR THE EGGS TOO MUCH, THEY WILL NOT COOK, AND IF YOU STIR THEM TOO LITTLE THEY WILL STICK TO THE PAN AND BURN. YOU NEED TO FIND THAT GOLDILOCKS LEVEL OF "JUST RIGHT."**

IN A SMALL BOWL, COMBINE THE ASPARAGUS, LEMON ZEST, LEMON OIL, AND CHIVES, AND SEASON WITH SALT AND PEPPER. SERVE THE DISH IN THREE PARTS ON PLATES. IN ONE THIRD, PLACE THE EGGS, IN ANOTHER 1/2 CUP OF THE SHAVED ASPARAGUS SALAD, AND THE LAST, THE TOASTED AND BUTTERED BAGUETTE. GARNISH THE EGGS WITH CHIVES AND BLACK PEPPER.

Egg White & Avocado Omelet

Makes 4 servings

In my early days of cooking, I learned how to make an omelet. At that time, I never thought of making an egg white omelet. As I've gotten older, I eat healthier – natural progression. This is a really simple, handsome, and healthy omelet, and it's an easy weekday breakfast or lunch.

---

2 avocados, peeled and pitted
8 egg whites, divided
Kosher salt and freshly ground black pepper
2 tablespoons plus 2 teaspoons unsalted butter, divided
2 teaspoons Lemon Oil (see page 60c), divided
Red pepper flakes, for garnish

Slice each avocado in half and thinly slice all of the halves.

In a small bowl, whisk 2 egg whites, seasoned with salt and pepper, until frothy.

In a medium nonstick pan over medium heat, warm 2 teaspoons of the butter. Once hot, add the egg whites, tilting the pan to evenly distribute them. Cook until the eggs are almost opaque, about 2 minutes.

With a soft heatproof spatula, release the egg whites from the pan, by running the spatula around the edge of the omelet. Fold one third of the omelet into itself, then roll it out onto a plate. Repeat with the remaining egg whites and butter.

Place an omelet onto each plate. Evenly divide and stagger the avocado slices among the plates next to the omelets, either forming them in a line or into the shape of a rose. Season them with salt and pepper, and drizzle about 1/2 teaspoon of lemon oil onto the avocados on each plate. Garnish the omelets with red pepper flakes.

Devilish Eggs

MAKES 2 TO 4 SERVINGS

DEVILED EGGS SEEM TO GO IN AND OUT OF FASHION IN RESTAURANTS AND BARS, SORT OF LIKE THE TRENDING OF CUPCAKES, BUT OF COURSE HOME COOKS ARE ALWAYS GOING TO MAKE BOTH. I REALLY LIKE HOW VERSATILE DEVILED EGGS ARE -- YOU CAN ADD BACON, CAVIAR, OR ANY NUMBER OF TASTY THINGS TO THEM. MY BEST DEVILED EGG ADVICE IS TO NEVER SKIP THE ICE-WATER BATH, AND THAT COMPLETE COOL DOWN OF THE EGGS, BEFORE YOU PEEL THEM. THAT STOPS THE COOKING, OF COURSE, BUT IT ALSO MAKES A HUGE DIFFERENCE IN TERMS OF REMOVING THE SHELLS. ALSO, DON'T LEAVE YOUR EGGS SITTING IN THAT WATER AFTER THEY'VE FULLY COOLED. THAT CAUSES THE MEMBRANE TO STICK TO THE SHELL, AND ALSO MAKES PEELING THEM TRICKY.

---

6 LARGE EGGS
3 TABLESPOONS MAYONNAISE
1 TEASPOON KOSHER SALT
1/2 TEASPOON FRESHLY GROUND BLACK PEPPER
1 TEASPOON MUSTARD POWDER
1 TEASPOON LEMON OIL (SEE PAGE 60C), FOR GARNISH
1 TEASPOON THINLY SLICED FRESH CHIVES, FOR GARNISH

OVER HIGH HEAT, BRING A MEDIUM POT OF WATER TO A BOIL.

ONCE BOILING, GENTLY ADD THE EGGS TO THE WATER AND MAINTAIN A SIMMER FOR 12 MINUTES.

USE A SLOTTED SPOON TO TRANSFER THE EGGS INTO AN ICE WATER-BATH TO COOL. ONCE COOLED, PEEL THE EGGS UNDER COLD RUNNING WATER THEN PAT DRY.

CUT THE EGGS IN HALF LENGTHWISE AND CAREFULLY TRANSFER THE YOLKS TO A SMALL BOWL. RINSE ANY YOLK OFF THE WHITES AND PAT DRY.

USING A SOFT SPATULA OR SOFT DOUGH SCRAPER, PUSH THE YOLKS THROUGH A FINE-MESH SIEVE INTO A MEDIUM BOWL. ADD THE MAYONNAISE, SALT, PEPPER, AND MUSTARD POWDER, AND MIX UNTIL SMOOTH.

PLACE THE FILLING IN A PIPING BAG, OR INTO A STURDY RESEALABLE PLASTIC BAG, AND SQUEEZE IT INTO ONE CORNER. THEN, USING SCISSORS, SNIP 1/2 INCH FROM THE CORNER OF THE BAG. PIPE THE FILLING EVENLY INTO EACH OF THE EGG WHITES. DRIZZLE WITH LEMON OIL AND GARNISH WITH CHIVES.

Vegetable-Loaded Frittata & Osetra Caviar

MAKES 2 TO 4 SERVINGS

I LIKE SERVING THIS FRITTATA AS A FAMILY-STYLE BRUNCH FOR FRIENDS AND FAMILY. IT'S A REALLY NICE DISH TO GATHER AROUND THE TABLE FOR. AND IT'S VERY COMFORTING. I USE OSETRA CAVIAR HERE, AS OPPOSED TO BELUGA, BECAUSE IT'S LESS SALTY AND HAS BETTER FLAVOR AND MORE BITE. THESE DAYS, CAVIAR COMES FROM EVERYWHERE -- THE COLUMBIA RIVER, ITALY, BULGARIA, AND CAVIAR FARMS ALL OVER THE WORLD -- BUT THE ORIGINAL CAVIAR CAME FROM THE CASPIAN SEA. IF YOU AREN'T SURE WHICH CAVIAR TO BUY, SIMPLY ASK SOMEONE AT YOUR MARKET TO HELP YOU.

1/4 CUP CELERY LEAVES, PLUS MORE FOR GARNISH
1 TABLESPOON PLUS 1 TEASPOON EXTRA-VIRGIN OLIVE OIL, DIVIDED
1 TABLESPOON FINELY DICED SHALLOT
1/2 CUP DICED ZUCCHINI
1/2 CUP ASPARAGUS TIPS (1-INCH PIECES)
3 LARGE EGGS
1/2 CUP CHERRY TOMATOES, QUARTERED
1 TEASPOON CHOPPED FRESH CHIVES
1/2 OUNCE OSETRA CAVIAR
KOSHER SALT AND FRESHLY GROUND BLACK PEPPER

PREHEAT THE OVEN TO 350 DEGREES F.

LIGHTLY TOSS THE CELERY LEAVES WITH 1 TEASPOON OF THE OLIVE OIL AND SET ASIDE.

IN A SMALL NONSTICK OVENPROOF PAN OVER MEDIUM HEAT, PREHEAT 1 TABLESPOON OF OLIVE OIL. ONCE HOT, ADD THE SHALLOT AND COOK FOR 2 TO 3 MINUTES, OR UNTIL TRANSLUCENT. ADD THE ZUCCHINI AND ASPARAGUS AND COOK, STIRRING OCCASIONALLY, FOR 2 TO 3 MINUTES.

MEANWHILE, IN A SMALL BOWL, WHISK THE EGGS UNTIL THEY ARE COMPLETELY HOMOGENOUS AND SMOOTH. ADD THE EGGS, CHERRY TOMATOES, AND CHIVES TO THE PAN. WITH A SOFT HEATPROOF SPATULA, STIR SLOWLY FOR 2 TO 3 MINUTES, OR UNTIL THE EGGS ARE VERY LIGHTLY SET BUT STILL WET AND JIGGLY. TRANSFER THE PAN TO THE OVEN AND BAKE FOR 2 TO 3 MINUTES, OR UNTIL THE EGGS ARE FULLY COOKED AND SET. REMOVE THE FRITTATA FROM THE OVEN AND USE THE SOFT HEATPROOF SPATULA TO SEPARATE IT FROM THE PAN.

TO SERVE, CAREFULLY SLIDE THE FRITTATA FROM THE PAN ONTO A WIDE PLATE. TOP IT WITH PINCHES OF CELERY LEAVES AND GARNISH WITH 1/2 OUNCE OF CAVIAR OF YOUR CHOICE.

Avocado Toast & Poached Egg

MAKES 2 TO 4 SERVINGS

When I'm not travelling, I make this breakfast at home, or some version of it, several times a week. It's healthy, tasty, and it plays well with all sorts of variations. For instance, if I have some smoked salmon in the fridge, I might top the avocado with that, or some nice, crispy bacon or turkey bacon. I tend to make my avocado toast at home with multigrain bread, but it's tasty with a bagel too, or whatever bread you have on-hand.

---

2 AVOCADOS, PEELED AND PITTED
1 TABLESPOON FRESHLY SQUEEZED LEMON JUICE
KOSHER SALT AND FRESHLY GROUND BLACK PEPPER
2 TABLESPOONS DISTILLED WHITE VINEGAR
4 LARGE EGGS
4 SLICES RUSTIC OR MULTIGRAIN BREAD, LIGHTLY TOASTED
1/4 CUP CHERRY TOMATOES, HALVED
1/2 JALAPENO, THINLY SLICED CROSSWISE

In a medium bowl, use the back of a fork to roughly mash the avocados with the lemon juice, and then season with salt and pepper.

Over high heat, bring a medium pot of water to a boil. Meanwhile, pour the vinegar into a medium bowl and gently crack the eggs into the bowl. Once the water comes to a boil, lower the heat to maintain a simmer. Use a slotted spoon to carefully slide one egg at a time into the water. Poach until the whites are set but the yolks are still runny, about 4 minutes. Use a slotted spoon to transfer the eggs to a bowl.

Evenly divide and top each slice of toast with the avocado mix. Evenly divide and arrange the tomato and jalapeno on top. Set one or two avocado toasts on each plate, and place an egg or two alongside each. Season the eggs with salt and pepper.

Over-Easy Eggs & Cantaloupe

MAKES 4 SERVINGS

IF YOU DON'T KNOW HOW TO PICK A GOOD, RIPE CANTELOUPE, ALL YOU NEED TO DO IS SMELL IT AND GIVE IT A LIGHT KNOCK WITH YOUR HAND. IF IT SMELLS DELICIOUS AND SOUNDS SOLID -- NOT HOLLOW -- YOU'VE GOT YOURSELF A GOOD ONE. WITH ALL OF MY RECIPES, I HOPE YOU HONOR THE SEASON AS BEST YOU CAN AND SOURCE TIP-TOP INGREDIENTS. WITH A RECIPE LIKE THIS, IT'S OF UTMOST IMPORTANCE, SINCE THERE ARE ONLY TWO PRIMARY INGREDIENTS.

ONE SMALL 2-POUND CANTALOUPE, QUARTERED AND SEEDED
2 TABLESPOONS UNSALTED BUTTER
8 LARGE EGGS
KOSHER SALT AND FRESHLY GROUND BLACK PEPPER

REMOVE THE PEEL FROM EACH WEDGE OF CANTALOUPE WHILE BEING CAREFUL TO KEEP THE PEEL INTACT. SET THE PEELS ASIDE, AND CUT EACH PIECE OF FRUIT INTO 1-INCH CUBES.

IN A LARGE NONSTICK PAN OVER MEDIUM HEAT, ADD THE BUTTER. ONCE HOT, CRACK THE EGGS INTO THE PAN. THEY SHOULD SIZZLE WHEN THEY HIT THE PAN. SEASON THE EGGS WITH SALT AND PEPPER. COOK THEM FOR 1 MINUTE, THEN CAREFULLY FLIP THEM. COOK FOR AN ADDITIONAL 1 MINUTE, UNTIL THE WHITE IS SET BUT THE YOLK IS STILL RUNNY.

SERVE 2 EGGS WITH EACH CANTALOUPE WEDGE. STAGGER THE SLICED CANTALOUPE CUBES ON THE PEELS.

Blueberry Pancakes & Compote

MAKES 4 TO 6 SERVINGS, 12 TO 14

THIS IS A VERY STRAIGHTFORWARD RECIPE AND IT NEVER DISAPPOINTS. MY BOYS ARE 16 AND 19 YEARS OLD AND THEY BOTH LOVE PANCAKES. WHEN THEY WERE GROWING UP, I'D OFTEN MAKE THEM FOR THEM ON THE WEEKENDS. OF COURSE, YOU CAN ADD OTHER INGREDIENTS BEYOND BLUEBERRIES TO THESE PANCAKES. SOMETIMES I LIKE TO ADD RASPBERRIES, AND ONE OF MY SONS REALLY LOVES CHOCOLATE CHIPS IN HIS. IF YOU GO THAT ROUTE, I RECOMMEND SCOOPING A LITTLE ICE CREAM ON TOP. WHY NOT?

BLUEBERRY COMPOTE

2 1/2 CUPS FRESH OR FROZEN BLUEBERRIES, DIVIDED
1/4 CUP WATER
1/3 CUP POWDERED SUGAR, PLUS MORE FOR DUSTING
1 (2-INCH) SLICE OF LEMON ZEST
1 TEASPOON FRESHLY SQUEEZED LEMON JUICE

PANCAKES

1 1/4 CUP ALL-PURPOSE FLOUR
2 TABLESPOONS SUGAR
1 1/2 TEASPOONS BAKING POWDER
3/4 TEASPOON BAKING SODA
1/2 TEASPOON KOSHER SALT
3/4 CUP BUTTERMILK
1/2 CUP SOUR CREAM
1 TEASPOON VANILLA EXTRACT
2 LARGE EGGS
4 TABLESPOONS UNSALTED BUTTER, MELTED, PLUS 3 TO 4 TABLESPOONS FOR COOKING
HIGH-QUALITY MAPLE SYRUP, FOR SERVING

IN A SMALL PAN OVER MEDIUM HEAT, ADD 1 CUP OF THE BLUEBERRIES, THE WATER, POWDERED SUGAR, LEMON ZEST, AND LEMON JUICE. SIMMER FOR 10 TO 12 MINUTES, STIRRING OCCASIONALLY, UNTIL MOST OF THE BERRIES HAVE BURST AND THE COMPOTE HAS REDUCED TO A THICK, GLOSSY SYRUP. SET ASIDE.

IN A LARGE BOWL, WHISK TOGETHER THE FLOUR, SUGAR, BAKING POWDER, BAKING SODA, AND SALT, MAKING SURE THERE ARE NO LUMPS.

IN A MEDIUM BOWL, WHISK TOGETHER THE BUTTERMILK, SOUR CREAM, VANILLA EXTRACT, EGGS, AND 4 TABLESPOONS OF MELTED BUTTER UNTIL FULLY INCORPORATED. FOLD THE BUTTERMILK MIXTURE INTO THE BOWL OF DRY INGREDIENTS. MIX TO INCORPORATE, BUT DO NOT OVERMIX. LET THE BATTER REST FOR ABOUT 10 MINUTES.

IN A MEDIUM NONSTICK PAN OVER MEDIUM HEAT, ADD 1 TABLESPOON OF BUTTER. ADD MORE BUTTER AS NEEDED BETWEEN BATCHES. ONCE HOT, MEASURE 1/3 CUP OF THE BATTER PER PANCAKE, AND POUR IT INTO THE PAN. EVENLY ADD 2 TO 3 TABLESPOONS OF BLUEBERRIES PER PANCAKE. AS THE PANCAKES BEGIN TO BUBBLE AND SET ON THE BOTTOM, AFTER 3 TO 4 MINUTES, FLIP THEM AND COOK FOR ANOTHER 2 TO 3 MINUTES, UNTIL GOLDEN BROWN.

LAYER 2 TO 3 PANCAKES ON EACH PLATE, TOP THEM WITH ABOUT 1/4 CUP WARM BLUEBERRY COMPOTE AND LIGHTLY DUST WITH POWDERED SUGAR. SERVE WITH A SIDE OF WARMED MAPLE SYRUP.

NOTE: IN ORDER TO KEEP YOUR PANCAKES WARM WHILE YOU COOK THEM PLACE ALREADY COOKED PANCAKES ON A HEATPROOF DISH IN THE OVEN AT 100 DEGREES F.

Eggs Benny

MAKES 4 SERVINGS

THIS IS A GREAT WEEKEND HANGOVER BREAKFAST, IF YOU STAYED OUT A LITTLE TOO LATE AND HAD ONE TOO MANY. IT'S ALSO REALLY EASY TO MAKE VEGETARIAN WITH SAUTEED SPINACH. OVER THE YEARS, INCLUDING MY BIGGER PRODUCTION YEARS AT THE WYNN AND THE BELLAGIO IN LAS VEGAS, I'VE MADE THOUSANDS OF PLATES OF EGGS BENEDICT. AT THE BELLAGIO, WE COOKED 1,000 BREAKFASTS EVERY MORNING. I'M GUESSING IF YOU MULTIPLIED 60 BENEDICTS A DAY -- MADE PERSONALLY BY ME -- BY 365 DAYS A YEAR, BY 16 YEARS THAT WOULD BE ROUGHLY HOW MANY I'VE COOKED IN MY LIFE. *A LOT.* JUST MAKE SURE THAT WHEN YOU MAKE THE HOLLANDAISE FOR THESE, YOU DON'T CRANK THE HEAT. IF YOUR HOLLANDAISE GETS TOO HOT IT WILL BREAK, AND THERE'S REALLY NO SOLUTION AT THAT POINT OTHER THAN TO START OVER.

---

4 EGG YOLKS
2 TEASPOONS FRESHLY SQUEEZED LEMON JUICE
2 TEASPOONS WATER
1/2 CUP CLARIFIED BUTTER
PINCH GROUND WHITE PEPPER
PINCH CAYENNE PEPPER
KOSHER SALT
8 SLICES CANADIAN BACON
4 TABLESPOONS DISTILLED VINEGAR, DIVIDED
8 LARGE EGGS, DIVIDED
4 ENGLISH MUFFINS, SPLIT, TOASTED, AND BUTTERED
3 TABLESPOONS THINLY SLICED CHIVES, FOR GARNISH

IN A HEATPROOF BOWL SET OVER A POT OF SIMMERING WATER, AND NOT TOUCHING THE WATER, WHISK THE EGG YOLKS, LEMON JUICE, AND WATER, UNTIL IT HAS DOUBLED IN VOLUME, ABOUT 2 TO 3 MINUTES. GRADUALLY ADD THE CLARIFIED BUTTER, CONTINUOUSLY WHISKING UNTIL THE SAUCE COMBINES AND THICKENS, ABOUT 4 MINUTES. ADD THE WHITE PEPPER AND CAYENNE, WHISK TO COMBINE, SEASON WITH SALT, AND SET ASIDE. IN A MEDIUM NONSTICK PAN OVER MEDIUM-HIGH HEAT, COOK THE CANADIAN BACON UNTIL GOLDEN BROWN ON BOTH SIDES AND CRISP AT THE EDGES, ABOUT 5 MINUTES. TRANSFER TO A PAPER TOWEL-LINED PLATE.

OVER HIGH HEAT, BRING A MEDIUM POT OF WATER TO A BOIL. MEANWHILE, POUR 2 TABLESPOONS OF VINEGAR INTO A MEDIUM BOWL AND GENTLY CRACK 4 EGGS INTO IT. ONCE THE WATER COMES TO A BOIL, LOWER THE HEAT TO MAINTAIN A SIMMER. USE A SLOTTED SPOON TO CAREFULLY SLIDE ONE EGG AT A TIME INTO THE WATER. POACH UNTIL THE WHITES ARE SET BUT THE YOLKS ARE STILL RUNNY, ABOUT 4 MINUTES. USE A SLOTTED SPOON TO TRANSFER THE EGGS TO A BOWL. REPEAT WITH THE REMAINING EGGS.

PLACE 2 TOASTED AND BUTTERED ENGLISH MUFFINS HALVES ONTO EACH PLATE. TOP EACH WITH A SLICE OF CANADIAN BACON, THEN A POACHED EGG. EVENLY DIVIDE AND SPOON THE WARM HOLLANDAISE SAUCE OVER EACH, AND GARNISH THEM ALL WITH CHIVES

Egg Drop Soup

Makes 4 to 6 servings

When I think of egg drop soup, I think of dining in so many different Chinese restaurants all over the world either late at night or early in the morning. That's when I most like to eat it. The chicken stock is very important to egg drop soup. It really needs to shine. So, either make mine (see page 10C), make your own with very good ingredients (don't rush!), or buy a high-quality broth. .

3/4 ounce (4 to 5 large) dried shiitake mushrooms
2 tablespoons grapeseed oil (or other neutral oil)
3 (1/4 -inch thick) slices peeled fresh ginger
6 scallions, green parts chopped into 1-inch pieces and white parts sliced, divided
3 fresh shiitake mushrooms, sliced
1 tablespoon toasted sesame oil
2 tablespoons toasted white sesame seeds
2 carrots, peeled and sliced (1/2-inch thick) crosswise
Freshly ground black pepper
1/4 cup tamari
2 quarts Chicken Stock (see page 10C), or good-quality store-bought chicken broth
1 1/2 cups chopped tomatoes
Kosher salt
1 tablespoon white wine vinegar
1 cup fresh or frozen peas
2 large eggs, beaten

Fill a medium pot with 4 cups of water, bring it to a boil over high heat, and remove from the heat. Add the dried shiitakes to the pot and fully submerge them under a smaller lid or plate. Let them steep for 40 to 50 minutes, until soft. Using a slotted spoon, remove the mushrooms from the pot, reserving the water, and discard.

In a medium pot over medium heat, warm the oil. Add the ginger, and cook for 1 to 2 minutes, or until fragrant. Add the scallion whites, fresh shiitakes, sesame oil, sesame seeds, carrots, and season with pepper to taste. Cook, stirring occasionally, for 4 to 5 minutes.

Add the tamari, the water from dried mushrooms, chicken stock, and chopped tomatoes. Cover, reduce heat to low and simmer for 12 to 15 minutes. Salt to taste.

Add the vinegar and peas. While quickly stirring, pour the eggs into the hot stock in a slow stream. Once fully incorporated continue stirring for about 2 more minutes. Remove and discard the ginger slices. Garnish each soup serving with scallion greens.

Egg Fried Rice

MAKES 4 SERVINGS

When making this fried rice be sure to get a nice bit of char going but do not burn your rice. That's always important with fried rice. This recipe is also kind of like my clean-the-fridge Chicken Chopped Salad (see page 22C). You can put whatever else you want into it. I make fried rice a lot at home, and that's in part because it's as good of a dish for one person as it is for a big gathering. In other words, it's easy to scale up or down

---

3 LARGE EGGS

3 TABLESPOONS SESAME OIL TOASTED, DIVIDED

1/4 CUP 1/4-INCH PEELED AND CUBED CARROTS

1/4 CUP GREEN BEANS, SLICED INTO 1/2-INCH PIECES

1/4 CUP FRESH OR FROZEN PEAS

1 TABLESPOON MINCED GARLIC

4 CUPS COLD COOKED WHITE RICE

2 TABLESPOONS SOY SAUCE

2 TEASPOONS SRIRACHA

2 TABLESPOONS OYSTER SAUCE

1/4 CUP THINLY SLICED SCALLION GREENS, FOR GARNISH

In a medium bowl, whisk the eggs until fully combined. In a large nonstick pan over medium heat, add 1 tablespoon of the sesame oil. Once hot, pour in the eggs. With a soft heatproof spatula, stir slowly and regularly. Cook for 4 to 5 minutes, until the eggs are set in custardy curds but still slightly runny. Transfer to a bowl, and set aside. Put the remaining sesame oil in the pan and return to medium heat. Once hot, add the carrots, green beans, and peas, and cook, stirring occasionally, for 2 to 3 minutes. Add the garlic and cook until aromatic, about 1 minute. Add the rice to the pan, breaking up any clumps as you stir it to coat it in the sesame oil. Cook for 1 to 2 minutes.

Meanwhile, in a small bowl, combine the soy sauce, Sriracha, and oyster sauce. Return the cooked egg to the fried rice and stir to evenly distribute. Pour the soy sauce mixture around the rim of the pan, and mix it in until combined. Remove from the heat.

Using a spoon, pack roughly one-quarter of the fried rice up to the rim of a small bowl. Take one of the plates you will serve the rice on, and place it over the packed bowl of rice. In one quick motion, flip the plate and bowl over, making sure to keep a tight grip on both. Set the plate down, give the bowl a few light taps, and slowly lift the bowl straight up. The rice should hold the form of the bowl. Garnish the fried rice with about 1 tablespoon of sliced scallions. Repeat with the remaining fried rice.

Seasonal Berries & Champagne Sabayon

MAKES 2 TO 4 SERVINGS

I GREW UP PICKING BLACKBERRIES IN A FIELD CLOSE TO MY CHILDHOOD HOME IN SCOTLAND, SO AS A KID I ATE A LOT OF SUN-WARMED, FRESH-OFF-THE-VINE BERRIES. I'VE ALWAYS LOVED THEM. IN THE SUMMER OF 1977, I STRAWBERRY PICKED IN THE NIAGARA FALLS REGION WHILE AT CULINARY SCHOOL. THEY PICKED US UP EVERY DAY AT 6AM BY BEEPING THE HORN. I'D RUN OUT AND JUMP ON THE BUS WITH ALL THE OTHER PICKERS. THEY DROVE US TO A FIELD WHERE WE HARVESTED ALL DAY, AND AT THE END OF THE DAY THEY PAID US $1 IN CASH FOR EVERY CASE. TRUTH BE TOLD, I PROBABLY LOST A FEW STRAWBERRIES EVERY DAY TO MY HUNGRY, YOUNG COOK MOUTH. THE BEST BERRIES ARE ALWAYS, OF COURSE, THE ONES YOU PICK YOURSELF. SECOND BEST ARE FARMERS MARKET BERRIES. IN TERMS OF THE BERRIES HERE, USE WHATEVER IS IN-SEASON AND MOST DELICIOUS WHEREVER YOU ARE.

---

8 EGG YOLKS
1 CUP SUGAR
3/4 CUP CHAMPAGNE
2 CUPS RIPE BERRIES, RINSED AND PATTED DRY
1 MEDIUM PEACH, RINSED AND SLICED
2 PASSION FRUITS, HALVED, FOR GARNISH.

FILL A DOUBLE BOILER WITH ABOUT 1 INCH OF WATER, AND PLACE IT OVER MEDIUM HEAT. IN THE TOP PAN OF A DOUBLE BOILER, OFF OF THE HEAT, WITH A METAL WHISK, LIGHTLY WHISK THE EGG YOLKS AND SUGAR UNTIL FULLY INCORPORATED.

NOTE: *IF YOU DON'T HAVE A PROPER DOUBLE BOILER AT HOME DON'T WORRY YOU CAN STILL MAKE THIS DISH. SIMPLY USE A METAL OR OTHER HEATPROOF BOWL THAT FITS SNUGLY OVER A MEDIUM POT OF SIMMERING WATER. JUST MAKE SURE THAT THE WATER DOESN'T COME IN CONTACT WITH THE BASE OF THE BOWL.*

WHEN THE WATER COMES TO A SIMMER, SET THE TOP PAN OVER THE SIMMERING BASE AND WHISK THE CHAMPAGNE INTO THE EGGS. CONTINUE VIGOROUSLY WHISKING, SCRAPING THE BASE OF THE PAN AS YOU GO FOR 6 TO 8 MINUTES, UNTIL THE SABAYON IS THICK AND CLINGS TO A SPOON.

NOTE: *IF THE SABAYON GETS TOO WARM AT ANY POINT REMOVE IT FROM THE DOUBLE BOILER FOR A BIT AND RETURN IT AFTER IT HAS SLIGHTLY COOLED.*

SET ASIDE AND COOL FOR 4 TO 5 MINUTES.
PLACE THE BERRIES AND SLICED PEACH ON A PLATTER AND POUR THE WARM SABAYON OVER THE TOP.

"GRANT HAS BEEN INVOLVED WITH NEW REALM BREWING FROM ITS INCEPTION. OUR PHILOSOPHY IS TO PAIR CRAFT BEER WITH LOCALLY SOURCED, SCRATCH FOOD. GRANT'S OVERSIGHT OF OUR KITCHEN DESIGN, MENU/RECIPE DEVELOPMENT AS WELL AS THE HIRING AND TRAINING OF OUR CULINARY TEAM HAS BEEN AN INTEGRAL PART OF OUR SUCCESS. HIS PROFESSIONAL CONTRIBUTIONS HAVE BEEN MEANINGFUL TO OUR BUSINESS. HIS EXPERTISE, CORE VALUES, AND FRIENDSHIP MEAN THE WORLD TO ME PERSONALLY".

CAREY FALCONE
CO-FOUNDER AND CEO, NEW REALM BREWING CO.

Very fresh eggs can be difficult to peel. Buy and refrigerate your eggs a week to 10 days in advance of cooking them to make peeling easier. This brief "breather" allows the eggs time to take in air, which helps separate the membranes from the shell.

Eggs TYPICALLY ARRIVE AT THE STORE 48-72 HOURS AFTER BEING LAID.

AT THE TIME OF THE FRENCH REVOLUTION, THE FRENCH ALREADY KNEW 685 DIFFERENT WAYS OF PREPARING EGGS.

IF THE NUMBER OF EGGS PRODUCED IN THE U.S. EVERY YEAR WERE LAID END-TO-END, THEY COULD CIRCLE THE EARTH AT ITS WIDEST POINT ALMOST 225 TIMES.

EGGS ARE ONE OF NATURE'S MOST PERFECT PROTEINS. EGGS PROVIDE A HIGH-QUALITY PROTEIN THAT IS OFTEN USED AS A STANDARD FOR COMPARING OTHER PROTEINS.

EGGS ARE A COMPLETE PROTEIN—MEANING THE PROTEIN IN AN EGG CONTAINS THE NINE ESSENTIAL AMINO ACIDS THAT OUR BODY CANNOT PRODUCE ON ITS OWN.

EGGS ARE ONE OF THE ONLY FOODS THAT NATURALLY CONTAIN VITAMIN D, A NUTRIENT THAT IS CRITICAL FOR BONE HEALTH AND IMMUNE FUNCTION.

No matter what your preference or budget, there is an EGG for everyone! America's EGG farmers produce EGGS from multiple housing systems – conventional, cage-free, free-range, and pasture-raised. No matter the housing system employed or type of EGG, the health and wellbeing of their hens is every EGG farmer's top priority — because healthy, well-cared-for hens lay EGGS!

EGG
PM

EGGSPM

Jean-Georges Vongerichten's Egg Caviar
Scotch Eggs & Caper Mustard Remoulade
Yorkshire Pudding
Brown Butter Herb Spaetzle
Buttermilk Hush Puppies
Linguini Carbonara
Cinnamon Swirl Bread Pudding
Grand Marnier Soufflé

Jean-Georges Vongerichten's Egg Caviar

MAKES 4 SERVINGS, 4 EGGS

This is one of Jean-Georges Vongerichten's most famous signature dishes that's served at quite a few of his restaurants. He's one of the world's most accomplished and talented chefs, with renowned restaurants all over the world. I'm honored to be friends with him. We've known each other since the late 1990s when we opened the Bellaggio Hotel & Casino, well, all of its restaurants, together in Las Vegas. Jean-Georges is all about sourcing and using the highest quality ingredients -- with absolutely no shortcuts -- to produce extremely healthy, well-balanced, inspired, and delicious food.

I've been lucky enough to eat at many of his restaurants over the years, especially the ones in New York. I've probably been to his Central Park restaurant Nougatine in the Trump International Hotel & Tower fifty times or more. This is an incredibly special and elevated egg dish -- a Jean-Georges Vongerichten signature dish that I've always adored. I'm excited for you to make it.

EGG

4 LARGE EGGS
1/4 TEASPOON OF KOSHER SALT
PINCH CAYENNE PEPPER
2 TABLESPOONS OF UNSLTED BUTTER

CREAM

1/2 CUP COLD HEAVY WHIPPING CREAM
SCANT 1/4 TEASPOON KOSHER SALT
PINCH CAYENNE PEPPER
1 TEASPOON VODKA
1 TEASPOON FRESHLY SQUEEZED LEMON JUICE

CAVIAR

4 TEASPOONS BELUGA, OSETRA, OR SEVRUGA CAVIAR, OR SALMON ROE

Use an egg topper to remove the top of each egg shell. Carefully pour the eggs into a medium bowl and reserve the shells. Whisk the eggs until fully combined. In a medium nonstick pan over medium heat, add the butter. Once hot, pour in the eggs. Whisk the eggs quickly and constantly for about 2 minutes, until they are very lightly curdled and still quite loose. Season with the salt and cayenne. Transfer to a small bowl, and set aside.

Over high heat, bring a medium pot of water to a boil. Once boiling, add the egg shells and boil for 3 to 4 minutes. Use a slotted spoon to transfer the shells to a plate. Gently remove the membranes from the inside of the shells. Pat the shells dry and place each in an egg cup. Spoon the scrambled eggs back into each shell leaving about an 1/8-inch of space at the top.

In the bowl of a stand mixer fitted with the whisk attachment, or in a large bowl over ice with a whisk, whip the cream for 3 to 4 minutes, until stiff peaks form. Season with the salt and cayenne pepper, and gently fold in the vodka and lemon juice. Fill a piping bag with the whipped cream.

Pipe the whipped cream in an open circle around the top of each eggshell filled with scrambled egg. Top each with 1 teaspoon of caviar in the middle of the whipped cream.

Serve each egg in its egg cup with a small espresso spoon. The idea here is to combine the warm eggs, the cool cream, and the salty caviar all in one bite.

EGG+CHICKEN

Scotch Eggs & Caper Mustard Remoulade

MAKES 4 SERVINGS

Growing up in Scotland, Scotch eggs were in all the pubs. It's a very British ploughman's platter sort of thing. If you go to a market anywhere in Great Britain on a Saturday or a Sunday they're going to be there. Scotch eggs are quite filling and I really do love them. The biggest potential downfall with these is overcooking them, so please don't. I guess you'll just have to drink another pint of lager if you do. Serve these with whatever type of sauce or condiment you want in addition to the remoulade. You can dip your Scotch eggs in ketchup or hot sauce if you want. That's not traditional but what do I care. With all of my recipes here in this book, I want you to feel free to add to them and make them your own.

REMOULADE

2 tablespoons Scottish whole grain mustard
1/2 teaspoon high-quality prepared horseradish (found in your grocer's refrigerator section)
1 teaspoon chopped fresh curly-leaf parsley
2 tablespoons capers, dried and toasted
1 tablespoon chopped shallots
1 dash Worcestershire sauce
1 tablespoon chopped dill pickle
1/4 cup mayonnaise
2 teaspoons white wine vinegar
Kosher salt and freshly ground black pepper

SCOTCH EGGS

6 large eggs, divided
1 cup whole milk
1 cup all-purpose flour
1 1/2 cups bread crumbs
2 tablespoons Old Bay Seasoning
3/4 pound ground pork
4 to 5 cups grapeseed oil (or other neutral oil)
Kosher salt and freshly ground black pepper
Chive oil to garnish

Preheat the oven to 350 degrees F.

In a small bowl, stir together the mustard, horseradish, parsley, capers, shallots, Worcestershire, pickle, mayonnaise, and vinegar until completely incorporated. Season with salt and pepper to taste, and then refrigerate until chilled. The remoulade keeps refrigerated for up to 3 days.

In a small, shallow bowl, lightly whisk 2 eggs with the milk. In another small shallow bowl, add the flour. In another small shallow bowl, combine the bread crumbs and Old Bay. Set all bowls aside. Bring a pot of water to a boil over high heat, then add the remaining 4 eggs and cook for 8 minutes. Use a slotted spoon to transfer the eggs into an ice water-bath to cool. Once cooled, peel the eggs under cold running water then pat dry.

Divide the sausage mixture into 4 portions; spread each one out into an oval shape. Add a boiled egg to the sausage, then gently form the sausage around the egg as evenly as possible. Do this for all of the eggs, and then put them on a plate and refrigerate uncovered for 3 to 4 minutes. Dredge each sausage-wrapped egg in the flour, shaking off the excess. Dip them in the beaten egg, letting any excess drip off. Roll them in the bread crumbs, coating well. Put the breaded eggs on a plate and refrigerate uncovered for 3 to 4 minutes. Heat about 1 inch of oil in a large Dutch oven or large, deep, heavy-bottomed pot with a thermometer attached to 375 degrees F.

Carefully fry the eggs for 3 to 4 minutes, turning occasionally, until they are golden brown. Using a slotted spoon or wire skimmer, transfer the eggs to a paper towel-lined plate to cool for 2 to 3 minutes. Move them to a parchment-lined baking sheet and bake for 5 to 6 minutes, or until the sausage is fully cooked. Check doneness with a toothpick. Spoon 3 to 4 tablespoons of the remoulade into the center of each plate. Carefully slice each Scotch egg in half lengthwise. Set one half of an egg cut side down in the remoulade and lean the other up against it. Season the eggs with salt and pepper, drizzle them with chive oil, and serve while still warm.

Yorkshire Pudding

MAKES 4 TO 6 SERVINGSS

I grew up eating Yorkshire pudding every Sunday. It's a very British and Scottish thing to serve with Sunday roast and my mother was good at making it. The roast, which was usually roast beef and occasionally lamb, might have been overcooked, who's to say, but the Yorkshire pudding never was. You can put herbs in these, use different types of flours for them, or add mustard but I usually don't. To me, Yorkshire pudding is like a peanut butter and jelly sandwich. It's best kept simple.

3/4 CUP ALL-PURPOSE FLOUR
1/2 TEASPOON KOSHER SALT
2 LARGE EGGS
1 CUP WHOLE MILK
1/4 CUP WATER
1 1/2 CUPS GRAPESEED OIL (OR OTHER NEUTRAL OIL)

Preheat the oven to 475 degrees F.

In a large bowl, combine the flour, salt, eggs, milk, and water and stir until smooth. Do not overmix. Cover and refrigerate the batter overnight (12 or more hours).

Place a standard 12-cup muffin tin onto a baking sheet and bake it, empty, for 5 minutes. Put 2 tablespoons of oil into each of the heated cups. Bake for another 5 minutes. Spoon the batter into the cups, filling them three-quarters full, and bake for 7 to 8 minutes. Reduce the temperature to 425 degrees F, and continue baking for 6 to 7 more minutes, or until the puddings are golden brown and crisp. Serve immediately.

Brown Butter Herb Spaetzle

MAKES 4 TO 6 SERVINGSS

THIS IS A EUROPEAN RECIPE – WITH ROOTS IN SWITZERLAND, AUSTRIA, ALSACE, AND GERMANY -- SO I NEVER REALLY HAD IT GROWING UP. THESE DAYS, I LOVE SPAETZLE AS A SOLID SIDE FOR A COZY FAMILY-STYLE MEAL CENTERED AROUND SOME SORT OF ROAST, LIKE POT ROAST OR ROASTED CHICKEN. DRINK WHATEVER YOU WANT THEM BUT I THINK A NICE, COLD IPA IS DELICIOUS WITH THESE CRISPY, BUTTERY NOODLES. IF YOU HAVE A SPAETZLE MAKER AT HOME, WONDERFUL, BUT IF NOT, SIMPLY USE A COLANDER WITH LARGER 1/4-INCH HOLES, ALONG WITH A SOFT SPATULA OR PLASTIC OR SILICONE DOUGH SCRAPER, TO MAKE THEM.

---

3 CUPS ALL-PURPOSE FLOUR
2 TEASPOONS KOSHER SALT
1 TEASPOON GROUND NUTMEG
2 LARGE EGGS
1/2 CUP PLUS 2 TABLESPOONS WHOLE MILK
1/2 CUP PLUS 2 TABLESPOONS SODA WATER
6 TABLESPOONS UNSALTED BUTTER, DIVIDED
2 TEASPOONS CHOPPED FRESH TARRAGON, DIVIDED
2 TEASPOONS CHOPPED FRESH CHIVES, DIVIDED
2 TEASPOONS CHOPPED FRESH CURLY PARSLEY, PLUS MORE FOR GARNISH
1 TEASPOON CHOPPED FRESH THYME, DIVIDED
KOSHER SALT AND FRESHLY GROUND BLACK PEPPER

IN A LARGE BOWL, WHISK TOGETHER THE FLOUR, SALT, AND NUTMEG, MAKING SURE THERE ARE NO LUMPS. ADD THE EGGS, MILK, AND SODA WATER, AND WHISK UNTIL FULLY INCORPORATED. LET THE BATTER REST FOR ABOUT 15 MINUTES.

OVER HIGH HEAT, BRING A LARGE POT OF WATER TO A BOIL. POUR 1 CUP OF BATTER INTO THE RESERVOIR OF THE SPAETZLE MAKER, PLACE IT OVER THE POT OF BOILING WATER, AND SLOWLY MOVE IT BACK AND FORTH OVER THE GRATE, SCRAPING WITH A RUBBER SPATULA TO CREATE 1-INCH-LONG SPAETZLE. IF YOU ARE USING A COLANDER WITH 1/4-INCH HOLES, PLACE IT OVER THE POT OF BOILING WATER. POUR 1 CUP OF BATTER INTO IT, AND USE A SOFT SPATULA OR DOUGH SCRAPER PRESS THE BATTER THROUGH THE HOLES TO CREATE 1-INCH-LONG SPAETZLE.

BOIL THE SPAETZLE FOR 2 MINUTES OR LONGER, STIRRING THEM ONCE OR TWICE TO SEPARATE THEM, AND UNTIL THEY FLOAT TO THE SURFACE. USE A SLOTTED SPOON TO TRANSFER THEM TO A PAPER TOWEL-LINED BAKING SHEET. CONTINUE THIS METHOD FOR THE REMAINING BATTER. IF THE BOIL WATER GETS STARCHY AT ANY POINT, START A NEW POT.

IN A MEDIUM NONSTICK PAN OVER HIGH HEAT, MELT 3 TABLESPOONS OF THE BUTTER. ADD HALF OF THE BOILED SPAETZLE TO THE PAN AND COOK FOR 4 TO 5 MINUTES, UNTIL THEY ARE GOLDEN BROWN. CAREFULLY FLIP AND COOK FOR ANOTHER 4 TO 5 MINUTES. TRANSFER TO A PLATE AND COOK THE REMAINING SPAETZLE THE SAME WAY.

IN A MEDIUM BOWL, ADD HALF OF THE COOKED SPAETZLE, ALONG WITH HALF OF EACH OF THE TARRAGON, CHIVES, PARSLEY, AND THYME. SEASON WITH SALT AND PEPPER. REPEAT WITH THE REMAINING SPAETZLE AND GARNISH IT ALL WITH PARSLEY.

Buttermilk Hush Puppies

MAKES 6 TO 8 SERVINGS, ABOUT 4 DOZEN

THESE HUSH PUPPIES ARE GREAT ON THEIR OWN AS A SNACK AND SIMPLY SPRITZED WITH SOME FRESH SQUEEZED LEMON, BUT IF YOU WANT A SAUCE FOR THEM, I RECOMMEND WHIPPING UP A NICE GARLICKY REMOULADE (SEE PAGE 50E), ADD GARLIC. CONNOR'S HUSH PUPPIES ALWAYS GO REALLY WELL WITH A FAMILY-STYLE SEAFOOD DINNER TOO. I THINK ADDING FRESH CORN TO THEM MAKES ALL THE DIFFERENCE, IN TERMS OF TEXTURE AND FLAVOR, SO PLEASE DON'T LEAVE IT OUT. IF YOU DON'T HAVE FRESH CORN, FROZEN IS FINE.

---

2 EARS YELLOW CORN, SHUCKED

4 CUPS PLUS 1 TABLESPOON GRAPESEED OIL (OR OTHER NEUTRAL OIL), DIVIDED

1 CUP CORNMEAL

1 1/2 CUPS ALL-PURPOSE FLOUR

3/4 TEASPOON BAKING POWDER

3/4 TEASPOON BAKING SODA

2 TEASPOONS KOSHER SALT, PLUS MORE FOR SEASONING

1/4 TEASPOON GROUND PAPRIKA

3/4 TEASPOON CAYENNE

1 TEASPOON SUGAR

1 CUP BUTTERMILK

1 LARGE EGG

4 TO 6 LEMON WEDGES, FOR GARNISH

SLICE THE KERNELS FROM THE COBS. IN A MEDIUM PAN OVER HIGH HEAT, PREHEAT 1 TABLESPOON OF THE OIL. ONCE IT'S HOT, ADD THE CORN AND COOK FOR ABOUT 2 MINUTES. TRANSFER THE CORN TO A PAPER TOWEL-LINED PLATE.

IN A MEDIUM BOWL, COMBINE THE CORNMEAL, FLOUR, BAKING POWDER, BAKING SODA, SALT, PAPRIKA, CAYENNE, AND SUGAR. IN A SEPARATE SMALL BOWL, COMBINE THE BUTTERMILK AND EGG, AND WHISK UNTIL COMBINED. POUR THE BUTTERMILK AND EGG MIX INTO THE CORNMEAL MIX AND STIR UNTIL FULLY INCORPORATED. FOLD IN THE COOKED CORN. REST THE BATTER AT ROOM TEMPERATURE COVERED OR FOR AT LEAST 1 HOUR BEFORE FRYING THE HUSH PUPPIES.

PREHEAT A DEEP FRYER OR LARGE HEAVY-BOTTOMED POT FILLED WITH THE REMAINING 4 CUPS OF GRAPESEED OIL TO 375 DEGREES F. USE TWO SMALL SPOONS TO SCRAPE AND CAREFULLY DROP THE HUSH PUPPY BATTER -- ABOUT 1 TABLESPOON PER PUP -- INTO THE HOT OIL. DO NOT OVERCROWD THEM; AIM FOR ABOUT 10 TO 12 AT A TIME. FRY TIME SHOULD BE ABOUT 2 TO 3 MINUTES. AS THE HUSH PUPPIES COOK AND TURN GOLDEN, USE A SLOTTED SPOON TO TRANSFER THEM TO A PAPER TOWEL-LINED PLATE. SEASON WITH SALT.

LINE A SHALLOW SERVING BOWL WITH A SQUARE OF GROCERY BAG BROWN PAPER. PLACE THE HUSH PUPPIES INTO THE LINED BOWL AND SERVE WITH LEMON WEDGES.

Linguini Carbonara

MAKES 4 SERVINGS

DON'T OVERCOOK YOUR PASTA! THAT'S REALLY MY ONLY ADVICE FOR THIS ONE. SO MANY PEOPLE DO, AND THEY END UP WITH A MUSHY CARBONARA. PLEASE DO NOT. THIS IS ONE OF MY FAVORITE DISHES FOR SHOWING OFF EGGS. IT'S SIMPLE, DELICIOUS, AND EVERYONE LOVES PASTA.

---

1 POUND DRIED LINGUINI
2 OUNCES PANCETTA, CHOPPED
2 TABLESPOONS FRESH OR FROZEN GREEN PEAS
4 EGG YOLKS, BEATEN
1 CUP GRATED PARMESAN, PLUS MORE FINELY GRATED FOR GARNISH
1 TEASPOON FRESHLY GROUND BLACK PEPPER
2 TEASPOONS STEMMED AND CHOPPED FRESH CURLY PARSLEY, PLUS MORE FOR GARNISH
KOSHER SALT AND FRESHLY GROUND BLACK PEPPER

OVER HIGH HEAT, BRING A LARGE POT OF SALTED WATER TO A BOIL. ADD THE LINGUINI AND COOK UNTIL AL DENTE.

MEANWHILE, PUT A SMALL PAN OVER MEDIUM HEAT. ONCE HOT, ADD THE PANCETTA AND COOK UNTIL BROWNED AND CRISP, 6 TO 8 MINUTES. TRANSFER THE PANCETTA TO A PAPER TOWEL-LINED PLATE. ADD THE PEAS TO THE PAN AND COOK FOR 1 TO 2 MINUTES. TRANSFER THE PEAS TO THE PLATE WITH THE PANCETTA.

IN A LARGE BOWL, MIX THE BEATEN EGG YOLKS, PARMESAN, PEPPER, PANCETTA, AND COOKED PEAS. WHEN THE LINGUINE IS DONE COOKING, USE A PAIR OF TONGS TO TRANSFER IT IMMEDIATELY FROM THE POT TO THE BOWL WITH THE EGG AND PARMESAN MIX. TURN THE LINGUINE WITH THE TONGS TO COAT IT IN THE EGG MIX. MOVE FAST SO THAT YOU USE THE HEAT OF THE PASTA TO COOK THE EGGS AND MELT THE CHEESE. ADD THE PARSLEY AND TOSS TO THOROUGHLY DISTRIBUTE. SEASON WITH SALT AND PEPPER TO TASTE. SERVE THE CARBONARA GARNISHED WITH MORE PARMESAN AND PARSLEY.

Cinnamon Swirl Bread Pudding

MAKES 4 TO 6 SERVINGS

You can get as creative as you want with this bread pudding, and you never have to worry about screwing it up. Add brandy or rum to it, or throw other dried fruit in. It's really just about combining the eggs and bread. In America, it seems like just about every chef has a recipe for bread pudding, in large part because it's an excellent way to use, and not waste, slightly past its prime bread. I recommend serving this bread pudding either straight-up or with ice cream, whipped cream, or crème anglaise.

1 cup heavy cream
1/3 cup whole milk
3 egg yolks
2 tablespoons sugar
Pinch kosher salt
Half loaf cinnamon swirl bread, sliced into 1-inch cubes
1/4 cup golden raisins
Powdered sugar, for dusting

Preheat the oven to 350 degrees F.

In a medium bowl, whisk the cream, milk, egg yolks, sugar, and salt for 1 to 2 minutes, until it becomes slightly frothy. Fold the bread and raisins into the custard mix.

Lightly butter a loaf pan or small Dutch oven. Pour the bread pudding into the pan and bake for about 40 minutes, until the pudding is cooked through and lightly browned. Set aside to cool for 3 to 5 minutes.

Sprinkle the top of the bread pudding with powdered sugar and caramelize it with a small blow torch or under a high temperature broiler. Serve family-style.

Grand Marnier Soufflé

MAKES 4 SERVINGS

IF YOU'RE TRYING TO IMPRESS YOUR WIFE OR HUSBAND, GIRLFRIEND OR BOYFRIEND, OR DATE WITH THIS DESSERT, YOU'LL SUCCEED. JUST BE SURE TO WHISK YOUR EGG WHITES TO TRUE SOFT PEAKS, AND DON'T FORGET TO BUTTER THOSE RAMEKINS. IF YOU DON'T DO BOTH THEN THE SOUFFLÉS WON'T RISE. YOU CAN USE OTHER LIQUEURS HERE IF YOU'D LIKE, TOO. I THINK IT ALSO TASTES GREAT WITH RASPBERRY OR CHOCOLATE LIQUEUR. THAT SAID, I LOVE THE FRENCH PERFUME OF GRAND MARNIER.

---

1 TABLESPOON UNSALTED BUTTER, FOR GREASING
2 TEASPOONS SUGAR
4 EGG YOLKS
1 TABLESPOON PLUS 1 TEASPOON POWDERED SUGAR, PLUS MORE FOR DUSTING
1 TEASPOON GRAND MARNIER
8 EGG WHITES

PREHEAT THE OVEN TO 400 DEGREES F AND ADJUST AN OVEN RACK TO THE MIDDLE POSITION.

LIGHTLY BUTTER FOUR, 3-INCH RAMEKINS. DUST WITH THE 2 TEASPOONS OF SUGAR, SHAKING OUT AND DISCARDING ANY EXCESS. FREEZE AND CHILL THE BUTTERED AND SUGARED RAMEKINS FOR ABOUT 1 HOUR.

IN A LARGE BOWL, WHISK 4 EGG YOLKS WITH THE POWDERED SUGAR AND GRAND MARNIER UNTIL INCORPORATED. IN ANOTHER LARGE BOWL, WHISK THE EGG WHITES UNTIL THEY REACH SOFT PEAKS. GENTLY FOLD THE WHITES INTO THE YOLK MIXTURE IN TWO BATCHES UNTIL JUST INCORPORATED. EVENLY DISTRIBUTE THE MIXTURE AMONG THE RAMEKINS, FILLING THEM TO THE RIM. PLACE THE RAMEKINS ON A BAKING SHEET AND BAKE FOR 10 MINUTES. THE SOUFFLÉS SHOULD RISE, TURN GOLDEN BROWN, AND NEARLY DOUBLE IN SIZE. DUST WITH POWDERED SUGAR, AND SERVE IMMEDIATELY.

EGGS ARE A NUTRITIONAL POWERHOUSE! ONE LARGE EGG HAS 6 GRAMS OF HIGH-QUALITY PROTEIN AND ALL 9 ESSENTIAL AMINO ACIDS, PLUS 6 OTHER ESSENTIAL VITAMINS AND MINERALS — ALL FOR 70 CALORIES. WHILE EGG WHITES HAVE SOME OF THE EGGS' HIGH-QUALITY PROTEIN, RIBOFLAVIN AND SELENIUM, THE MAJORITY OF AN EGG'S NUTRIENT PACKAGE (AND NEARLY HALF OF ITS PROTEIN) IS FOUND IN THE YOLK.

E

THE EGG IS USED AROUND THE WORLD AS A SYMBOL OF THE START OF NEW LIFE AND THEY ARE GIVEN TO CELEBRATE EASTER OR SPRINGTIME.

SINCE BIRDS AND EGGS PRECEDED MAN IN THE EVOLUTIONARY CHAIN, THEY'VE EXISTED LONGER THAN HISTORIANS. EAST INDIAN HISTORY INDICATES THAT WILD FOWL WERE DOMESTICATED AS EARLY AS 3200 B.C. EGYPTIAN AND CHINESE RECORDS SHOW THAT FOWL WERE LAYING EGGS FOR MAN IN 1400 B.C.

EGG+CHICKEN

In 1980, Grant and I were cooks giving away free chicken wings to the bartender in exchange for free jugs of beer and smoking under the exhaust hood at the illustrious Beacon Motor Inn in Jordan, Ontario,Canada. Little did we know that he would go on to journey across the world fulfilling a dream and honing his culinary talent.

His passion for fine food shows through again in this cookbook of his, exploring the principal ingredients of eggs and chicken. Which came first, who knows, but Grant's recipes will make you want to eat both. Bon Appetite!

Life long best friend
Rick Buerger
Phuket, Thailand

Bill's Daily Breakfast on the Shoot

EGG+CHICKEN

RESEARCH ALSO SHOWS THAT EATING BREAKFAST IS A MARKER FOR OVERALL HEALTH AND GOOD BEHAVIOR IN SCHOOL CHILDREN. BREAKFAST EATERS ARE LESS LIKELY TO MISS SCHOOL DUE TO ILLNESS OR OTHER ISSUES, AND ARE LESS LIKELY TO BE TARDY TO CLASS.

A HEN REQUIRES BETWEEN 24 TO 26 HOURS TO PRODUCE AN EGG. AFTER THE EGG IS LAID, THE HEN STARTS ALL OVER AGAIN IN ABOUT 30 MINUTES.

THE COLOR OF AN EGG'S SHELL IS DETERMINED BY THE HEN'S EAR LOBE. HENS WITH WHITE FEATHERS AND EAR LOBES LAY WHITE-SHELLED EGGS; HENS WITH RED FEATHERS AND EAR LOBES LAY BROWN EGGS.

DID YOU KNOW: THERE IS NO NUTRITIONAL DIFFERENCE BETWEEN WHITE AND BROWN EGGS?

Grant MacPherson brought Celtic flair to his Executive Chef role at Sandy Lane. He showed great innovation through his recruitment and management of staff. Grant's culinary skills and international experience have left his hallmark on our Menus at Sandy Lane.

Irish Owner of Sandy Lane Hotel, Barbados
Dermot Desmond

EGG

E

Hard-boiled eggs are easiest to peel after cooling. Cooling causes the egg to contract slightly in the shell. To peel, gently tap the egg on your countertop until the shell is finely cracked all over, then roll it between your hands to loosen the shell. Peel starting at the large end and hold the egg under cold running water to help ease the shell off.

EGGS PROVIDE VARYING AMOUNTS OF SEVERAL *B* VITAMINS REQUIRED FOR THE PRODUCTION OF ENERGY IN THE BODY, SUCH AS THIAMIN, RIBOFLAVIN, FOLATE, *B12* AND *B6*.

EGGS ARE RICH IN THE ESSENTIAL AMINO ACID LEUCINE (ONE LARGE EGG PROVIDES 600 MG), WHICH PLAYS A UNIQUE ROLE IN STIMULATING MUSCLE PROTEIN SYNTHESIS.

EGGS ARE ONE OF THE MOST AFFORDABLE SOURCES OF COMPLETE PROTEIN AVAILABLE.

EGG+CHICKEN

C

DID YOU KNOW YOU CAN SCRATCH THE SURFACE OF A BROWN EGG AND CREATE A DESIGN IN THE SHELL?

AN EGGSHELL HAS FROM 7,000-17,000 TINY PORES DISTRIBUTED OVER THE SHELL SURFACE, WITH A GREATER NUMBER AT THE LARGE END.

HAVE YOU EVER TRIED PUTTING A RAW EGG IN A GLASS OF VINEGAR? ADD SOME FOOD COLORING TO WHITE VINEGAR, COMPLETELY SUBMERGE A RAW EGG AND WATCH WHAT HAPPENS OVER THE NEXT 24 TO 36 HOURS. (SPOILER: THE SHELL WILL DISAPPEAR AND YOU WILL HAVE A "SHELL-LESS" EGG.)

GROWTH HORMONES ARE NEVER GIVEN TO EGG-LAYING HENS OR CHICKS, PER FOOD & DRUG ADMINISTRATION (FDA) REGULATIONS.

ALL EGGS SOLD FOR HUMAN CONSUMPTION ARE ANTIBIOTIC FREE. WHEN SICK HENS ARE GIVEN ANTIBIOTICS, ANY EGGS THAT ARE LAID ARE DIVERTED FROM HUMAN CONSUMPTION, PER FDA REGULATIONS.

CHICKEN

AM

ChickenAM

Chicken Congee & Chinese Doughnut Sticks
Chicken Stock
Chicken Ramen, Soy Sauce Eggs & Pork Belly
Cornflake-Crusted Chicken & Waffles
Malaysian Chicken Satay & Peanut Sauce
Shredded Chicken Lettuce Wraps
Fully-Loaded Chicken Burger
Chicken Chopped Salad
Chicken Caesar & Quinoa Crackers
Teriyaki Chicken, Baby Bok Choy & Lotus Root Chips
Matzo Ball Soup
Buffalo Chicken Lollipops & Blue Cheese Fondue
Bang Bang Chicken Wings
Chicken Liver Pâté & Lemony Cherry Sauce
Chicken Paillard

Chicken Congee & Chinese Doughnut Sticks

MAKES 4 TO 6 SERVINGS

Congee is primarily a jet lag dish for me when I'm overseas. I love it when I'm tired and a bit out of sorts. It's extremely comforting. Traditionally congee is just rice and water, but I think chicken adds a lot to it. Over my years of traveling, I've seen so many high rollers, gamblers, and others night owls enjoy it immensely in the morning. I get it. You can put raw egg or century egg in my congee if you want. I think both are really tasty additions.

---

4 cups Chicken Stock (see page 10c), or good-quality store-bought chicken broth
4 cups water plus 2 tablespoons, divided
1 cup jasmine rice, rinsed
12 ounces skinless, boneless chicken breast (about 2 medium breasts), thinly sliced
1 tablespoon oyster sauce
2 teaspoons cornstarch
2 tablespoons grapeseed oil (or other neutral oil)
1 (1-inch) piece peeled fresh ginger, thinly sliced
4 cloves garlic, minced
2 scallions (both white and green parts), thinly sliced
Kosher salt and freshly ground black pepper
2 Chinese doughnut sticks, or 2 pieces toasted crusty bread
Fried shallots, for garnish
Cilantro, stemmed and chopped, for garnish
Chili oil

In a large pot over medium heat, bring the chicken stock and 4 cups of water to a boil. Once boiling, add the rice and stir. Cover the pot, bring back to a boil and cook for 30 to 40 minutes, stirring occasionally, until the congee is thickened and creamy.

Meanwhile, in a medium bowl combine the sliced chicken with the oyster sauce, cornstarch, and remaining water, and stir until fully incorporated. Add the oil and stir. Add the sauced chicken to the pot and simmer for 2 to 3 minutes. Add the ginger, garlic, and scallions, and season with salt and pepper. Stir for 1 to 2 minutes and then serve hot in bowls along with the Chinese doughnut sticks. Garnish with the fried shallots, cilantro, and chili oil.

Chicken Stock

MAKES 4 QUARTS

MY CHICKEN STOCK WILL MAKE ANY DISH YOU ADD IT TO BETTER INCLUDING THE BOOK'S CHICKEN CONGEE & CHINESE DOUGHNUT STICKS (SEE PAGE 8C), CHICKEN RAMEN, SOY SAUCE EGGS & PORK BELLY (SEE PAGE 12C), EGG DROP SOUP (SEE PAGE 34E), MATZO BALL SOUP (SEE PAGE 28C), SCOTTISH CHICKEN PIE (SEE PAGE 44C), AND BEER-CAN CHICKEN FEAST (SEE PAGE 56C). IT'S SLOW-SIMMERED GOODNESS WITH MUCH LESS SODIUM, AND A SIGNIFICANTLY CLEANER TASTE, THAN ANY BROTH YOU CAN FIND AT THE STORE.

---

2 CHICKEN CARCASSES
6 QUARTS WATER
1 UNPEELED WHITE ONION, HALVED
1 CARROT, ROUGHLY CHOPPED
4 CELERY RIBS, ROUGHLY CHOPPED
1 FENNEL BULB, ROUGHLY CHOPPED
5 SPRIGS FRESH THYME
1/4 CUP PARSLEY STEMS
2 BAY LEAVES
1 TABLESPOON BLACK PEPPERCORNS

OVER HIGH HEAT, BRING A LARGE STOCKPOT, FILLED HALFWAY WITH WATER TO A BOIL. ADD THE CHICKEN CARCASSES TO THE BOILING WATER AND SIMMER FOR ABOUT 5 MINUTES. USE TONGS TO TRANSFER THE CHICKEN CARCASSES TO A BAKING SHEET. DISCARD THE WATER AND ADD 6 QUARTS OF FRESH WATER TO THE STOCKPOT. RETURN THE CARCASSES TO THE POT, ALONG WITH THE ONION, CARROT, CELERY, FENNEL, THYME, PARSLEY, BAY LEAVES, AND PEPPERCORNS.

PUT THE POT OVER HIGH HEAT AND BRING TO A BOIL. REDUCE HEAT TO MEDIUM-LOW AND SIMMER UNCOVERED FOR ABOUT 4 HOURS. THE STOCK SHOULD REDUCE BY ABOUT A THIRD. REMOVE IT FROM THE HEAT AND SET ASIDE TO COOL FOR ABOUT 1 HOUR. STRAIN THE STOCK, DISCARDING THE BONES, VEGETABLES, HERBS, AND SPICES. COVER AND REFRIGERATE OVERNIGHT (12 OR MORE HOURS). REMOVE AND DISCARD THE SOLIDIFIED FAT ON TOP. TIGHTLY COVER AND REFRIGERATE FOR UP TO 1 WEEK, OR FREEZE FOR UP TO 6 WEEKS.

Chicken Ramen, Soy Sauce Eggs & Pork Belly

MAKES 4 SERVING

RAMEN IS A ONE-BOWL MEAL, AND IT'S TYPICALLY SERVED IN JAPAN FOR BREAKFAST OR LUNCH. I TEND TO THINK OF IT AS ASIAN CHICKEN NOODLE SOUP, ALTHOUGH THERE ARE ENDLESS VARIATIONS. AT ITS CORE, IT'S A DEEPLY COMFORTING HOME-STYLE DISH. I'VE DONE QUITE A BIT OF TRAVELLING AND WORKING IN JAPAN IN MY LIFE, AND SOME OF THAT INSPIRED THE RAMEN BAR THAT I OPENED IN 2017 IN WYNN PALACE LAS VEGAS. OVER THE YEARS, I'VE COME TO FEEL THAT THE QUALITY OF RAMEN HINGES ON THE BROTH AND THE SOY SAUCE EGG, SO PLEASE TAKE CARE WITH BOTH. I DON'T LOUDLY SLURP MY NOODLES AS THEY DO IN JAPAN, BUT I REALLY LOVE THAT PEOPLE DO, AND I LIKE TO HEAR IT. I THINK THAT LOUD SLURPING ULTIMATELY STEMS FROM THE SENSE OF EXCITEMENT ABOUT THE MEAL. IT'S ALL PART OF THE ENJOYMENT. SO, SLURP AWAY.

---

4 LARGE EGGS
2 CUPS PLUS 3 TABLESPOONS SOY SAUCE, DIVIDED
1 TABLESPOON UNTOASTED SESAME OIL
1 1/2 TABLESPOONS MINCED FRESH GINGER
2 TABLESPOONS MINCED GARLIC
4 CUPS CHICKEN STOCK (SEE PAGE 10), OR GOOD-QUALITY STORE-BOUGHT CHICKEN BROTH
8 SCALLIONS, GREEN PARTS CHOPPED INTO 1-INCH PIECES
1 CUP SLICED FRESH SHIITAKE MUSHROOMS
KOSHER SALT
8 (4-INCH WIDE, 1/4-INCH-THICK) SLICES PORK BELLY (ABOUT 1 POUND)
24 OUNCES FRESH RAMEN NOODLES, BOILED UNTIL AL DENTE
1 TO 2 SCALLIONS (BOTH WHITE AND GREEN PARTS), THINLY SLICED FOR GARNISH

OVER HIGH HEAT, BRING A MEDIUM POT OF WATER TO A BOIL. ONCE THE WATER COMES TO A BOIL, USE A SLOTTED SPOON TO CAREFULLY SLIDE ONE EGG AT A TIME INTO THE WATER. LOWER THE HEAT TO MAINTAIN A SIMMER FOR 8 MINUTES. USE A SLOTTED SPOON TO TRANSFER THE EGGS TO AN ICE WATER-BATH TO COOL. ONCE COOLED, GENTLY PEEL THE EGGS UNDER COLD RUNNING WATER, PAT DRY, AND PLACE IN A MEDIUM BOWL. ADD 2 CUPS OF THE SOY SAUCE TO THE BOWL, AND TOP THE EGGS WITH SOMETHING LIGHT TO GENTLY SUBMERGE THEM. A SMALL ZIP-TOP PLASTIC BAG FILLED WITH ENOUGH WATER WORKS GREAT. COVER AND REFRIGERATE OVERNIGHT (12 OR MORE HOURS).

IN A LARGE POT OVER MEDIUM HEAT, HEAT THE SESAME OIL. ONCE HOT, ADD THE GINGER AND GARLIC, AND COOK FOR 1 TO 2 MINUTES, UNTIL FRAGRANT. ADD THE REMAINING SOY SAUCE AND COOK FOR ABOUT 1 MINUTE. ADD THE STOCK, SCALLION GREENS, AND SHIITAKE MUSHROOMS, AND BRING TO A BOIL. LOWER THE HEAT AND SIMMER FOR ABOUT 15 MINUTES. SEASON WITH SALT TO TASTE.

PUT A LARGE NONSTICK PAN OVER HIGH HEAT. ONCE HOT, ADD THE SLICED PORK BELLY TO THE PAN AND COOK FOR ABOUT 3 MINUTES, UNTIL IT STARTS TO BROWN AND COLOR. THE SLICES SHOULD SIZZLE A LOT WHEN THEY HIT THE PAN AND THROUGHOUT COOKING. FLIP AND COOK FOR ANOTHER 3 TO 4 MINUTES. TRANSFER THE PORK BELLY TO A PAPER TOWEL-LINED PLATE.

EVENLY DIVIDE THE COOKED NOODLES AMONG 4 BOWLS. LADLE 1 CUP OF HOT STOCK AND SHIITAKES OVER THE NOODLES AND EGGS. DRAIN THE EGGS, SLICE EACH ONE IN HALF LENGTHWISE AND SET TWO HALVES ON TOP OF EACH BOWL. ARRANGE 2 SLICES OF PORK BELLY ON TOP OF EACH BOWL, ALONGSIDE THE EGG, AND GARNISH WITH SLICED SCALLIONS.

Cornflake-Crusted Chicken & Waffles & Slaw

MAKES 4 SERVING

THIS IS A QUINTESSENTIAL WEEKEND COMFORT DISH. I REALLY LIKE THE DIFFERENT TEXTURES YOU GET WITH IT, ESPECIALLY THE CRISPINESS OF THE CHICKEN, AND THE SOFT AND CHEWY BITE OF THE WAFFLES. I'M MORE INCLINED TO COOK UP PANCAKES AT HOME THAN WAFFLES, BUT I DO CRAVE WAFFLES EVERY NOW AND AGAIN. WHEN I DO, THIS DISH REALLY HITS THE SPOT.

4 CUPS GRAPESEED OIL (OR OTHER NEUTRAL OIL)
2 CUPS GRATED CABBAGE
1/4 CUP GRATED CARROTS
1/3 CUP MAYONNAISE
2 TABLESPOONS RED WINE VINEGAR
2 TABLESPOONS CHOPPED FRESH CURLY OR FLAT-LEAF PARSLEY
KOSHER SALT AND FRESHLY GROUND BLACK PEPPER
8 PIECES OF SKINLESS, BONE-IN CHICKEN (4 LEGS, 4 THIGHS)
2 1/4 CUPS ALL-PURPOSE FLOUR, DIVIDED
5 LARGE EGGS, DIVIDED
4 CUPS CORNFLAKES, CRUSHED
2 TABLESPOONS SUGAR
1 1/2 TEASPOONS BAKING POWDER
3/4 TEASPOON BAKING SODA
1/2 TEASPOON KOSHER SALT
1 1/4 CUPS BUTTERMILK
6 TABLESPOONS UNSALTED BUTTER, MELTED
1 TEASPOON VANILLA EXTRACT
NONSTICK COOKING SPRAY
HONEY, FOR DRIZZLING

PREHEAT A DEEP FRYER OR LARGE HEAVY-BOTTOMED POT FILLED WITH THE GRAPESEED OIL TO 375 DEGREES F.

IN A LARGE BOWL, TOSS THE CABBAGE AND CARROTS. IN A SMALL BOWL, WHISK THE MAYONNAISE, VINEGAR, AND PARSLEY. SEASON WITH SALT AND PEPPER. TOSS THE CABBAGE AND CARROTS WITH THE DRESSING AND SET ASIDE.

OVER HIGH HEAT, BRING A LARGE POT OF WATER TO A BOIL. ADD THE CHICKEN TO THE BOILING WATER AND BOIL FOR ABOUT 5 MINUTES. USE TONGS TO TRANSFER THE CHICKEN TO A PAPER-TOWEL LINED BAKING SHEET AND PAT DRY.

ON A LARGE PLATE, ADD 1 CUP OF THE FLOUR. IN A MEDIUM SHALLOW BOWL, BEAT 3 OF THE EGGS. ON ANOTHER LARGE PLATE, ADD THE CRUSHED CORNFLAKES. DREDGE ALL OF THE CHICKEN PIECES IN THE FLOUR, SHAKING OFF THE EXCESS. DIP THEM IN THE EGGS, LETTING ANY EXCESS DRIP OFF. COAT THEM IN THE CORNFLAKES.

FRY THE ENCRUSTED CHICKEN IN A FEW SMALL BATCHES, DO NOT OVERCROWD THEM, FOR 3 TO 4 MINUTES, UNTIL GOLDEN BROWN. USE TONGS TO TRANSFER THE CHICKEN TO A PAPER TOWEL-LINED BAKING SHEET. WHEN ALL OF THE CHICKEN HAS BEEN FRIED, REMOVE AND DISCARD THE PAPER TOWELS.

IN A LARGE BOWL, WHISK TOGETHER THE REMAINING FLOUR, SUGAR, BAKING POWDER, BAKING SODA, AND 1/2 TEASPOON OF SALT, MAKING SURE THERE ARE NO LUMPS. IN A MEDIUM BOWL, WHISK TOGETHER THE REMAINING EGGS, BUTTERMILK, MELTED BUTTER, AND VANILLA EXTRACT UNTIL FULLY INCORPORATED. SLOWLY WHISK THE BUTTERMILK MIXTURE INTO THE BOWL OF DRY INGREDIENTS. WHISK TO INCORPORATE BUT DO NOT OVERMIX. LET THE BATTER REST FOR ABOUT 10 MINUTES. PREHEAT YOUR FAVORITE WAFFLE IRON TO MEDIUM-HIGH, AND LIGHTLY OIL IT WITH THE COOKING SPRAY. POUR 1 1/2 CUPS OF BATTER INTO THE IRON BASED ON ITS SIZE. CLOSE THE TOP AND COOK FOR 4 OR 5 MINUTES, OR UNTIL GOLDEN BROWN AND CRISPY. TRANSFER THE WAFFLE TO THE OVEN RACK TO KEEP WARM, AND REPEAT WITH THE REMAINING BATTER.

TO SERVE, SET ONE WAFFLE OFF-CENTER ON EACH PLATE. PLACE COLESLAW ACROSS FROM THE WAFFLE AND LEAN 2 PIECES OF CHICKEN AGAINST EACH WAFFLE. DRIZZLE EVERYTHING IN HONEY

Malaysian Chicken Satay & Peanut Sauce

MAKES 4 TO 6 SERVINGS, 12 SKEWERS

THIS WAS ONE OF MY FAVORITE DISHES WHEN I LIVED IN MALAYSIA IN THE LATE 1990S, OPENING ONE HOTEL AND RUNNING ANOTHER. SATAY IS A WILDLY DELICIOUS AND UBIQUITOUS STREET FOOD OVER THERE, THAT'S POPULAR AT ALL TIMES OF DAY. I ATE A LOT OF IT DURING THOSE YEARS. BE SURE TO GET YOUR PAN RIPPING HOT WHEN YOU SEAR THE CHICKEN SKEWERS BECAUSE THAT'S HOW YOU DEVELOP SIGNIFICANT COLOR AND FLAVOR.

SATAY

1 TABLESPOON MINCED LEMONGRASS (FROM 1 PLUMP STALK OF LEMONGRASS, TENDER WHITE INNER BULB ONLY)
1 TABLESPOON GROUND CORIANDER
1 TABLESPOON GROUND CUMIN
1 TABLESPOON GROUND GINGER
1 TABLESPOON GROUND TURMERIC
4 SKINLESS, BONELESS CHICKEN THIGHS, SLICED INTO 1-INCH CUBES (35 TO 40 PIECES)
1 TABLESPOON GRAPESEED OIL (OR OTHER NEUTRAL OIL)

PEANUT SAUCE

2 TABLESPOONS GRAPESEED OIL (OR OTHER NEUTRAL OIL)
1 TABLESPOON PLUS 1 TEASPOON MINCED SHALLOT
1 TABLESPOON MINCED GINGER
1 TABLESPOON MINCED LEMONGRASS (FROM 1 PLUMP STALK OF LEMONGRASS, TENDER WHITE INNER BULB ONLY)
1 TABLESPOON CHILI PASTE
1 TABLESPOON MINCED FRESH GALANGAL
1/2 TEASPOON GROUND TURMERIC
1/3 CUP WATER
1 TABLESPOON SUGAR
1/2 TEASPOON KOSHER SALT
1 CUP RAW PEANUTS, ROUGHLY CHOPPED

SLICED CUCUMBER
DICED RED ONION

IN A SMALL BOWL, MIX TOGETHER THE LEMONGRASS, CORIANDER, CUMIN, GINGER, AND TURMERIC. EVENLY RUB THE SPICE MIX ALL OVER THE CHICKEN. REFRIGERATE COVERED FOR 6 TO 12 HOURS.

IN A MEDIUM POT OVER HIGH HEAT, ADD 2 TABLESPOONS OF THE OIL FOR THE PEANUT SAUCE. ONCE HOT, ADD THE SHALLOT AND COOK, STIRRING OCCASIONALLY, FOR ABOUT 2 MINUTES, OR UNTIL SOFT. ADD THE GINGER AND LEMONGRASS, AND COOK FOR ABOUT 2 MINUTES, UNTIL AROMATIC. ADD THE CHILI PASTE, GALANGAL, TURMERIC, WATER, SUGAR, SALT, AND PEANUTS. REDUCE THE HEAT TO LOW AND SIMMER FOR 1 1/2 HOURS, UNTIL THE SAUCE THICKENS AND TURNS A DEEPER SHADE OF BROWN. SET ASIDE.

THREAD 3 TO 4 PIECES OF MARINATED CHICKEN ONTO EACH 12-INCH SKEWER, ARRANGING THEM QUITE CLOSE TOGETHER. IN A MEDIUM HEAVY-BOTTOMED PAN OVER HIGH HEAT, ADD REMAINING TABLESPOON OF OIL. ONCE HOT, SEAR THE CHICKEN SKEWERS, A FEW AT A TIME, FOR 2 TO 3 MINUTES ON EACH SIDE, UNTIL NICELY BROWNED AND COOKED THROUGH.

SEASON THE SKEWERS SALT AND PEPPER TO TASTE. SERVE THEM HOT ALONG WITH THE WARM PEANUT SAUCE, CUCUMBER, AND RED ONION.

EGG+CHICKEN

Shredded Chicken Lettuce Wraps

MAKES 4 SERVINGS

THIS RECIPE IS A GREAT WAY TO MAKE USE OF LEFTOVER CHICKEN. SO, IF YOU MAKE THE BEER-CAN CHICKEN (SEE PAGE 56C), DIDN'T INVITE ENOUGH PEOPLE OVER TO ENJOY IT, AND HAVE SOME LEFTOVERS, GO AHEAD AND SHRED IT FOR THESE. THESE WRAPS ARE THE PERFECT OUTDOOR POOLSIDE OR PICNIC FOOD, BECAUSE YOU DON'T NEED UTENSILS, THEY'RE LIGHT AND YUMMY, AND YOU GET TO EAT THEM BY HAND. THEY ALSO GO REALLY WELL WITH A COLD BEER, SHANDY, OR SPRITZER -- OR SOMETHING ELSE THAT'S EQUALLY LIGHT AND REFRESHING. ENJOY!

---

14 SKINLESS, BONELESS CHICKEN THIGHS
KOSHER SALT AND FRESHLY GROUND BLACK PEPPER
1/4 CUP SOY SAUCE
2 TEASPOONS SRIRACHA
1 TEASPOON MINCED GARLIC
1 TEASPOON MINCED GINGER
1 TABLESPOON SCALLIONS (BOTH WHITE AND GREEN PARTS), THINLY SLICED
1 PACK THIN DRIED GLASS (MUNG BEAN THREAD) NOODLES
1 HEAD BUTTER LETTUCE, RINSED, LEAVES BROKEN APART
1/4 CUP ROASTED PEANUTS
1 FRESNO CHILI, THINLY SLICED

PREHEAT THE OVEN TO 375 DEGREES F.

PLACE THE CHICKEN ON A FOIL-LINED BAKING SHEET AND SEASON IT WITH SALT AND PEPPER. BAKE FOR 25 TO 30 MINUTES, UNTIL THE CHICKEN THIGHS REACH AN INTERNAL TEMPERATURE OF 165 DEGREES F. SET ASIDE TO COOL UNTIL WARM. WHILE STILL WARM, SHRED THE CHICKEN, AND SET ASIDE.

IN A SMALL BOWL, MIX TOGETHER THE SOY SAUCE, SRIRACHA, GARLIC, GINGER, AND SCALLIONS. SET ASIDE FOR AT LEAST 1 HOUR SO THAT THE FLAVORS MELD.

PUT THE GLASS NOODLES IN A MEDIUM HEATPROOF BOWL. OVER HIGH HEAT, BRING A MEDIUM POT OF WATER TO A BOIL. ONCE BOILING, REMOVE FROM HEAT AND POUR OVER THE GLASS NOODLES. LET STEEP FOR 10 TO 15 MINUTES, OR UNTIL THE NOODLES ARE SOFT. DRAIN THE NOODLES, RETURN THEM TO THE BOWL AND COVER WITH COLD WATER.

PAT DRY 8 MEDIUM-SIZED LEAVES OF BUTTER LETTUCE. TO ASSEMBLE THE WRAPS, PUT ABOUT 2 TABLESPOONS OF PATTED-DRY GLASS NOODLES, THEN A FEW PIECES OF SHREDDED CHICKEN ONTO EACH LEAF. TOP EACH WRAP WITH 1 TO 2 TEASPOONS OF ROASTED PEANUTS, AND A SLICE OF FRESNO CHILI. PUT THE SAUCE IN A SMALL SELF-SERVE DISH ON THE SIDE, FOR SPOONING INTO THE WRAPS.

Fully-Loaded Chicken Burger

MAKES 4 SERVINGS

I FEEL THE SAME WAY ABOUT A CHICKEN BURGER PATTY AS I DO ABOUT ANY BURGER PATTY, OR MEATBALL FOR THAT MATTER -- LESS IS MORE. I DON'T LIKE TOO MUCH FILLER IN THEM IN TERMS OF EGG, BREAD CRUMBS AND ANYTHING ELSE. SEASON THE PATTY JUST A BIT AND THAT'S THAT. LET THE MEAT SHINE. FEEL FREE, HOWEVER, TO ADD OTHER THINGS AS TOPPERS AND SAUCES TO THIS BURGER, LIKE A CILANTRO MAYO OR A TOMATO CONFIT. WHATEVER SOUNDS GOOD.

---

12 OUNCES SKINLESS, BONELESS CHICKEN LEGS, CUT INTO 2-INCH PIECES

12 OUNCES SKINLESS, BONELESS CHICKEN BREAST, CUT INTO 2-INCH PIECES

2 TABLESPOONS MINCED FRESH GINGER

2 TABLESPOONS MINCED GARLIC

1/4 CUP CHOPPED FLAT-LEAF PARSLEY

KOSHER SALT AND FRESHLY GROUND BLACK PEPPER

2 TABLESPOONS GRAPESEED OIL (OR OTHER NEUTRAL OIL), DIVIDED

1/4 CUP MAYONNAISE

2 TABLESPOONS KETCHUP

1 TABLESPOON UNSALTED BUTTER

4 LARGE EGGS

4 SESAME BURGER BUNS, TOASTED

16 BREAD AND BUTTER PICKLES

1 CUP LOOSELY PACKED STEMMED ARUGULA LEAVES

4 THINLY SLICED PIECES VERMONT CHEDDAR CHEESE

IN THE BOWL OF A FOOD PROCESSOR, COMBINE THE CHICKEN, GINGER, AND GARLIC, AND PULSE FOR 1 TO 2 MINUTES, UNTIL THE MEAT IS COARSELY GROUND. TRANSFER THE MEAT TO A MEDIUM BOWL, AND FOLD IN THE PARSLEY, AND SEASON WITH SALT AND PEPPER.

LINE A LARGE PLATE OR PLATTER WITH WAXED PAPER. FORM FOUR 6-OUNCE CHICKEN PATTIES AND PLACE THEM ON IT. IN A MEDIUM NONSTICK PAN OVER MEDIUM-HIGH HEAT, ADD 1 TABLESPOON OF THE OIL. ONCE HOT, PLACE TWO PATTIES INTO THE PAN AND COOK THEM, FLIPPING ONCE, UNTIL BROWNED AND COOKED THROUGH, FOR 8 TO 10 MINUTES. TRANSFER THE PATTIES TO A PAPER TOWEL-LINED PLATE. REPEAT WITH THE REMAINING PATTIES.

IN A SMALL BOWL, COMBINE THE MAYONNAISE AND KETCHUP UNTIL FULLY BLENDED.

IN A LARGE NONSTICK PAN OVER MEDIUM HEAT, ADD THE BUTTER. ONCE HOT, CRACK THE EGGS INTO PAN. THEY SHOULD SIZZLE WHEN THEY HIT THE PAN. SEASON THE EGGS WITH SALT AND PEPPER. COOK THEM FOR 1 MINUTE, THEN CAREFULLY FLIP THEM. COOK FOR AN ADDITIONAL 1 MINUTE, OR UNTIL THE WHITE IS SET BUT THE YOLK IS STILL RUNNY. TRANSFER TO A PLATE.

SPREAD 1 HEAPING TABLESPOON OF THE MAYONNAISE KETCHUP MIXTURE ON THE TOP OF EACH BUN, AND PLACE 4 PICKLES AND 1/4 CUP OF ARUGULA ON THE BOTTOM OF EACH BUN. SET THE BURGER PATTIES ON TOP OF THE ARUGULA AND PICKLES, AND COMPLETE EACH BURGER BY TOPPING THE PATTIES WITH A SLICE OF CHEDDAR, THEN THE FRIED EGG, AND FINALLY THE TOP BUN.

Chicken Chopped Salad

MAKES 4 SERVINGS

This is a family-style recipe that also works really well in a buffet. I think of this as a sort of clean-the-fridge salad, meaning you can throw other ingredients into it if you have them. Things that could work nicely here are olives, capers, cucumbers etc. Be free and creative.

---

1 EAR YELLOW CORN, SHUCKED
1/4 CUP EXTRA-VIRGIN OLIVE OIL PLUS 2 TEASPOONS, DIVIDED
1 SKIN-ON, BONE-IN CHICKEN LEG
1 SKIN-ON, BONE-IN CHICKEN BREAST
KOSHER SALT AND FRESHLY GROUND BLACK PEPPER
2 HEADS ICEBERG LETTUCE
1 AVOCADO, CUBED
1/2 CUP THINLY SLICED RADISHES
1/2 CUP JULIENNED CARROT
1/2 CUP ALMONDS, TOASTED
2 TABLESPOONS SHERRY VINEGAR
1 TEASPOON DIJON MUSTARD
1/2 TEASPOON WATER

Preheat the oven to 350 degrees F.

Slice the kernels from the cob. In a small pan over high heat, preheat 2 teaspoons of the oil. Once hot, add the corn and cook for about 2 minutes. Transfer the corn to a paper towel-lined plate.

Place the chicken onto a foil-lined baking sheet and season with salt and pepper. Bake for 35 to 40 minutes, until the chicken breasts reach an internal temperature of 165 degrees F. Set aside to cool. Once cooled, remove the skin, shred the chicken by hand, and set aside.

Chop the iceberg lettuce into 1/2-inch-wide pieces. In a large bowl, combine the lettuce, avocado, corn, radishes, carrots, almonds, and shredded chicken.

In a medium jar, combine the remaining olive oil with the sherry vinegar, Dijon mustard, and water, and season with salt and pepper. Top with a lid and shake vigorously until fully combined.

Pour the dressing over the salad, lightly toss, and serve family-style.

Chicken Caesar & Quinoa Crackers

MAKES 4 SERVINGS

IF YOU HAVE A SOUS VIDE SET-UP AT HOME THEN I HIGHLY RECOMMEND USING THAT TO COOK THE CHICKEN BECAUSE IT PERFECTLY COOKS THE BREASTS AND KEEPS THEM NICE AND JUICY. SET YOUR SOUS VIDE TO 160 DEGREES F, SEASON THE CHICKEN, AND COOK IT FOR ABOUT ONE HOUR BEFORE TRANSFERRING IT TO AN ICE BATH FOR 3 TO 4 MINUTES. THEN CARRY ON WITH THE RECIPE. I THINK THE WORST THING YOU CAN DO TO ANY CAESAR SALAD IS OVERDRESS IT. THAT'S WHY I'VE GIVEN YOU JUST ENOUGH DRESSING HERE TO ACCENTUATE THE ROMAINE BUT NOT DROWN IT.

DRESSING

1 ANCHOVY FILLET
1 CLOVE GARLIC, FINELY GRATED OR POUNDED WITH A PINCH OF SALT
1 TEASPOON FRESHLY SQUEEZED LEMON JUICE
1 TEASPOON DIJON MUSTARD
1/2 TEASPOON WHITE WINE VINEGAR
1/2 TEASPOON WORCESTERSHIRE SAUCE
2 SHAKES TABASCO SAUCE
1 EGG YOLK
1 CUP EXTRA-VIRGIN OLIVE OIL
KOSHER SALT AND FRESHLY GROUND BLACK PEPPER

CHICKEN & SALAD & QUINOA CHIPS

2 SKINLESS, BONELESS CHICKEN BREASTS
KOSHER SALT AND FRESHLY GROUND BLACK PEPPER
1 TABLESPOON EXTRA-VIRGIN OLIVE OIL
1/2 CUP QUINOA
1 CUP WATER
1 LARGE EGG
2 BABY ROMAINE LETTUCE HEADS, HALVED INTO WEDGES
SHAVED PARMESAN CHEESE, FOR GARNISH
CHIVE OIL, FOR GARNISH

PREHEAT THE OVEN TO 350 DEGREES F.

COARSELY CHOP THE ANCHOVY AND THEN POUND IT INTO A FINE PASTE. IN A MEDIUM BOWL, STIR TOGETHER THE ANCHOVY, GARLIC, LEMON JUICE, MUSTARD, VINEGAR, WORCESTERSHIRE SAUCE, AND TABASCO. BEAT IN THE EGG YOLK WITH A FORK, THEN SLOWLY ADD THE OLIVE OIL, CONTINUING TO BEAT, UNTIL FULLY INCORPORATED AND SMOOTH. SEASON WITH SALT AND PEPPER.

SEASON THE CHICKEN BREASTS WITH SALT AND PEPPER. IN A MEDIUM PAN OVER MEDIUM HEAT, PREHEAT THE OLIVE OIL. ONCE HOT, ADD THE CHICKEN AND COOK FOR 3 TO 4 MINUTES, THEN FLIP. COOK FOR AN ADDITIONAL 3 TO 4 MINUTES, OR UNTIL THE CHICKEN IS COOKED THROUGH AND THE JUICES RUN CLEAR. TRANSFER TO A PLATE, AND SET ASIDE. ONCE COOLED, SLICE EACH BREAST IN HALF EVENLY.

IN A SMALL POT OVER HIGH HEAT, ADD THE QUINOA AND WATER, AND BRING TO A BOIL. ONCE BOILING, COVER THE POT, AND LOWER THE HEAT TO MAINTAIN A SIMMER FOR 12 TO 15 MINUTES, OR UNTIL THE QUINOA IS FULLY COOKED AND THE IS WATER ABSORBED. REMOVE FROM THE HEAT AND LET STAND, COVERED, FOR 5 MINUTES. FLUFF THE QUINOA WITH A FORK.

IN THE BOWL OF A BLENDER OR FOOD PROCESSOR, COMBINE THE COOLED QUINOA AND EGG, AND LIGHTLY BLEND UNTIL PUREED BUT STILL SLIGHTLY CHUNKY. LINE A BAKING SHEET WITH PARCHMENT PAPER OR A SILICONE MAT. EVENLY SPREAD THE QUINOA MIX ONTO THE BAKING SHEET USING AN OFFSET OR SOFT SPATULA. BAKE FOR ABOUT 30 MINUTES UNTIL THE QUINOA IS CRISP AND DRY. IF IT IS NOT YET DRY, CONTINUE BAKING IN 5-MINUTE INCREMENTS. REMOVE FROM THE OVEN, AND SET ASIDE TO COOL. ONCE COOLED, BREAK INTO 2-INCH CHIPS.

PLACE A ROMAINE WEDGE ONTO EACH PLATE. DRIZZLE ABOUT 2 TABLESPOONS OF DRESSING OVER EACH WEDGE. GARNISH WITH PARMESAN SHAVINGS AND QUINOA CHIPS. PLACE A SLICE OF CHICKEN NEXT TO EACH ROMAINE WEDGE. DRIZZLE CHIVE OIL AROUND ALL SALADS.

Teriyaki Chicken, Baby Bok Choy & Lotus Root Chips

MAKES 4 SERVINGS

I started making teriyaki chicken when I lived in Vancouver B.C. because there were quite a lot of talented Japanese cooks in the kitchen who I learned from. I love the sweet glaze of it and how the marinade adds so much flavor to the chicken. My older son, Graeme, asks for this dish a lot. It's easy to whip up, and I bet you'll like it as much as him.

---

4 SKINLESS, BONELESS CHICKEN BREASTS

2 CUPS PLUS 3 TABLESPOONS GRAPESEED OIL, DIVIDED

1/4 MEDIUM SWEET ONION, CHARRED

1 LARGE CARROT, CHARRED

2 STALKS CELERY, CHARRED

2 CUPS WATER

2 1/4 CUPS SOY SAUCE, DIVIDED

1/4 CUP SAKE

1/8 CUP MIRIN

1/4 CUP MINCED GARLIC, DIVIDED

2 TABLESPOONS PLUS 1 TEASPOON MINCED PEELED FRESH GINGER

1 TABLESPOON HONEY

1/2 POUND CHICKEN BONES

1/4 CUP SUGAR

1 TEASPOON CORNSTARCH

4 HEADS OF BABY BOK CHOY, CLEANED AND TRIMMED

1 MEDIUM LOTUS ROOT, PEELED

KOSHER SALT

PREHEAT THE OVEN TO 375 DEGREES F.

LINE A BAKING SHEET WITH FOIL, PLACE THE CHICKEN BREASTS ON IT, BRUSH 1 TABLESPOON OF THE OIL EVENLY ALL OVER THEM, AND SEASON WITH SALT AND PEPPER. ROAST FOR 20 MINUTES, OR UNTIL THE INTERNAL TEMPERATURE REACHES 165 DEGREES F.

ON STOVETOP, GRILL, OR IN OVEN, COOK THE ONION, CARROT AND CELERY OVER HIGH HEAT FOR 4 TO 5 MINUTES UNTIL NICELY CHARRED.

IN A LARGE POT OVER HIGH HEAT, COMBINE WATER, 2 CUPS OF THE SOY SAUCE, SAKE, MIRIN, CHARRED ONION, CHARRED CARROT, CHARRED CELERY, 3 TABLESPOONS OF GARLIC, 2 TABLESPOONS OF GINGER, HONEY, AND CHICKEN BONES. BRING TO A BOIL THEN REDUCE HEAT TO LOW AND SIMMER FOR 20 MINUTES. ADD SUGAR AND CORNSTARCH, AND STIR WELL TO ELIMINATE ANY CLUMPS. STRAIN THE SAUCE THROUGH A FINE-MESH SIEVE INTO A MEDIUM BOWL.

IN A SMALL BOWL, COMBINE THE REMAINING SOY SAUCE, GINGER, AND GARLIC. SLICE EACH HEAD OF BOK CHOY IN HALF LENGTHWISE.

IN A LARGE NONSTICK PAN OVER HIGH HEAT, ADD 2 TABLESPOONS OF GRAPESEED OIL. ONCE HOT, PLACE BOK CHOY SLICED-SIDE-DOWN IN THE HOT OIL. COOK FOR ABOUT 3 MINUTES, FLIP, ADD THE SOY MIXTURE, AND COOK FOR ABOUT 2 MORE MINUTES, UNTIL CRISP-TENDER.

PREHEAT A DEEP FRYER OR HEAVY-BOTTOMED POT FILLED WITH THE REMAINING 2 CUPS OF GRAPESEED OIL TO 375 DEGREES F.

USING A MANDOLIN OR A SHARP KNIFE THINLY SLICE THE LOTUS ROOT CROSSWISE. CAREFULLY PUT THE LOTUS SLICES INTO THE HOT OIL, DO NOT OVERCROWD THEM, AND FRY FOR 1 TO 2 MINUTES, OR UNTIL GOLDEN AND CRISP. TRANSFER TO A PAPER TOWEL-LINED BAKING SHEET AND SEASON WITH SALT.

TO SERVE, PLACE TWO HALVES OF THE BABY BOK CHOY ONTO EACH PLATE SLICED-SIDE-UP. PLACE A CHICKEN BREAST ON TOP OF THE BOK CHOY AND SPOON THE WARM TERIYAKI SAUCE ON TOP AND AROUND. GARNISH WITH THE FRIED LOTUS ROOT CHIPS.

Matzo Ball Soup

MAKES 4 SERVINGS

Working in any hotel restaurant, I think you should always have matzo ball soup on the menu, especially during the holidays. It's a regularly requested soup nationally, much like chicken noodle soup. Matzo balls are really a type of dumpling in my mind, much like an Austrian knödel. I highly recommend making my Chicken Stock (see page 10C) for this traditional and festive soup.

3/4 cup matzo meal
3 large eggs, beaten
4 tablespoons grapeseed oil (or other neutral oil), divided
1/2 teaspoon baking powder
3 tablespoons water
Kosher salt and freshly ground black pepper
1 tablespoon minced garlic
1/4 yellow onion, chopped
2 stalks celery, chopped
2 carrots, peeled and chopped
3 quarts Chicken Stock (see page 10), or good quality store-bought chicken broth
2 skinless, boneless chicken thighs
2 cups elbow macaroni
2 tablespoons chopped flat-leaf parsley

In a medium bowl, combine the matzo meal, eggs, 3 tablespoons of oil, baking powder, water, and season with salt and pepper. Cover with plastic wrap and refrigerate for about 1 hour to hydrate. Using dampened hands, roll the matzo mixture into 4 balls, each about 2 inches in diameter. Transfer them to a plate.

In a large pot over medium heat, add the remaining 1 tablespoon of oil. Once hot, add the garlic, onions, celery, and carrots, and cook for 10 to 12 minutes, until the onions are translucent. Add the stock and chicken to the pot, and bring it to a boil. Reduce the heat to low and simmer for about 30 minutes. Use a slotted spoon to transfer the cooked chicken to a plate and set aside to cool. Add the elbow macaroni and matzo balls to the pot and lightly simmer for about 20 minutes, until cooked through.

Meanwhile, shred the chicken.

Place an equal amount of shredded chicken into each bowl, then add 1 matzo ball to each. Ladle the broth and vegetables into each bowl, and garnish with the chopped parsley.

Buffalo Chicken Lollipops & Blue Cheese Fondue

MAKES 4 TO6 SERVINGS

REGIONAL DISH, THEY'RE NOW POPULAR COAST TO COAST. BE SURE TO SHARPEN YOUR KNIFE BEFORE YOU SET INTO THIS RECIPE BECAUSE WHEN YOU TRIM THE CHICKEN YOU WANT TO KEEP THE CUTS CLEAN AND GO ALL THE WAY TO THE BONE.

BLUE CHEESE FONDUE

5 TABLESPOONS UNSALTED BUTTER, DIVIDED
1 CUP BUTTERMILK
1/4 CUP BLUE CHEESE
1/4 CUP CREAM CHEESE
1 TEASPOON FINELY CHOPPED FRESH ROSEMARY LEAVES
KOSHER SALT AND FRESHLY GROUND BLACK PEPPER

CHICKEN LOLLIPOPS

4 CUPS GRAPESEED OIL (OR OTHER NEUTRAL OIL)
24 CHICKEN DRUMETTES (ABOUT 3 POUNDS), TRIMMED OR FRENCHED INTO LOLLIPOPS
1 CUP FRANK'S ORIGINAL REDHOT, DIVIDED
2 MEDIUM CARROTS, PEELED AND SLICED INTO STICKS
2 MEDIUM CELERY RIBS, TRIMMED AND SLICED INTO STICKS

PREHEAT A DEEP FRYER OR LARGE HEAVY-BOTTOMED POT FILLED WITH THE 4 CUPS OF GRAPESEED OIL TO 375 DEGREES F.

IN A SMALL POT OVER MEDIUM HEAT, MELT 1 TABLESPOON OF THE BUTTER FOR THE FONDUE. ADD THE BUTTERMILK, CONTINUE STIRRING, AND BRING IT TO A BOIL. REDUCE THE HEAT TO LOW, AND ADD THE BLUE CHEESE, CREAM CHEESE, AND ROSEMARY. STIR UNTIL THE CHEESE HAS MELTED. SEASON WITH SALT AND PEPPER AND SET ASIDE.

RINSE THE CHICKEN WINGS AND PAT DRY. FRY THE CHICKEN IN SMALL BATCHES, DO NOT OVERCROWD THEM, FOR 8 TO 10 MINUTES, UNTIL THEY ARE COOKED THROUGH, GOLDEN BROWN, AND CRISPY. USE A SLOTTED SPOON TO TRANSFER THEM TO A PAPER-TOWEL LINED BAKING SHEET.

IN A SMALL PAN OVER MEDIUM HEAT, COMBINE THE FRANK'S ORIGINAL REDHOT WITH THE REMAINING 4 TABLESPOONS OF BUTTER, AND STIR UNTIL THE BUTTER HAS MELTED. IN A LARGE BOWL, ADD THE CHICKEN AND SAUCE AND TOSS TO EVENLY COAT.

SERVE THE WINGS DRIZZLED WITH A SPOONFUL OF THE WARM BLUE CHEESE FONDUE, ALONG WITH CARROT AND CELERY STICKS.

Bang Bang Chicken Wings

MAKES 4 SERVINGS

THESE WINGS ARE A REALLY FUN AND YUMMY SNACK TO SERVE TO LOVED ONES. THEY'RE EASY TO EAT AND I LOVE HOW NICE AND CRISPY THEY GET. I TEND TO LIKE WINGETTES AND DRUMETTES BOTH EQUALLY, BUT MY OLDER SON, GRAEME, HAS ALWAYS PREFERRED WINGETTES. WE CALL THEM FLATS. I DEDICATE THIS RECIPE TO HIM.

---

24 CHICKEN WINGETTES (ABOUT 3 POUNDS)
1 TABLESPOON EXTRA-VIRGIN OLIVE OIL
KOSHER SALT AND FRESHLY CRACKED BLACK PEPPER
1/2 CUP SOY SAUCE
1/2 CUP OYSTER SAUCE
2 TABLESPOONS SRIRACHA
2 TEASPOONS FRESHLY SQUEEZED LEMON JUICE
CURLY PARSLEY, CHOPPED, FOR GARNISH
1 (1-INCH) PIECE PEELED FRESH GINGER, JULIENNED, FOR GARNISH

PREHEAT THE OVEN TO 375 DEGREES F.

RINSE THE CHICKEN WINGS AND PAT DRY. IN A LARGE BOWL, MIX THE CHICKEN WITH THE OLIVE OIL AND LIGHTLY SEASON WITH SALT AND PEPPER. TRANSFER THE CHICKEN TO A FOIL-LINED BAKING SHEET AND ROAST FOR 20 TO 25 MINUTES, UNTIL COOKED THROUGH AND GOLDEN BROWN.

MEANWHILE, IN A SMALL POT, COMBINE THE SOY SAUCE, OYSTER SAUCE, SRIRACHA, AND LEMON JUICE, AND BRING TO A BOIL OVER HIGH HEAT. STIR THE SAUCE, REDUCE THE HEAT TO LOW, AND SIMMER FOR 10 TO 12 MINUTES, UNTIL THE SAUCE HAS SLIGHTLY THICKENED.

WITH A LARGE SPOON DIVIDE THE SAUCE EVENLY AMONG 4 PLATES, PLACING IT IN THE CENTER, AND PUT 6 WINGS ON TOP OF EACH. GARNISH WITH PARSLEY AND GINGER.

Chicken Liver Pâté & Lemony Cherry Sauce

MAKES 4 TO 6 SERVINGS, 1 TERRINE

I'VE ALWAYS BEEN A FAN OF PÂTÉ. OVERALL, IT WAS A LOT MORE POPULAR IN THE 1980S THAN IT IS NOW, BUT IT'S A CLASSIC DISH AND ALWAYS WILL BE. MY PÂTÉ IS REALLY SMOOTH, SOFT, SPREADABLE, AND EASY TO EAT. IT'S A SPECIAL HOLIDAY TIME, CELEBRATORY FOOD FOR ME. DON'T SKIP THE SIMMERED CHERRIES. THEY ADD A REALLY NICE, BRIGHT ACIDITY THAT CUTS THROUGH THE RICHNESS OF THE PÂTÉ.

---

2 1/2 STICKS UNSALTED BUTTER, DIVIDED
1 CUP CHICKEN LIVERS, PATTED DRY AND TRIMMED
1 SHALLOT, SLICED
1 SPRIG FRESH THYME
3 EGG YOLKS
1 CUP CHERRIES, PITTED
2 TABLESPOONS RED WINE VINEGAR
1/4 CUP WATER
1 LEMON, ZESTED
3 TABLESPOONS SUGAR
SEVERAL PIECES MELBA TOAST, OR THINLY SLICED AND TOASTED BAGUETTE

IN A MEDIUM POT OVER LOW HEAT, MELT 2 STICKS OF THE BUTTER. ONCE MELTED, ADD THE CHICKEN LIVERS, SHALLOT, AND THYME, AND COOK FOR 10 TO 12 MINUTES, STIRRING OCCASIONALLY, UNTIL THE CHICKEN LIVERS ARE SOFT. REMOVE FROM THE HEAT AND DISCARD THE THYME.

IN THE BOWL OF A BLENDER OR FOOD PROCESSOR, ADD THE CHICKEN LIVER MIX AND EGG YOLKS, AND SALT AND PEPPER TO SEASON, PUREE UNTIL SMOOTH.

USING A SOFT SPATULA OR DOUGH SCRAPER, PUSH THE BLENDED CHICKEN LIVER MIX THROUGH A FINE-MESH SIEVE INTO A 1-QUART TERRINE OR SOUFFLÉ DISH. TAP THE DISH ON THE COUNTER A FEW TIMES TO REMOVE ANY AIR BUBBLES. COVER AND REFRIGERATE FOR ONE HOUR.

IN A SMALL POT OVER LOW HEAT, MELT THE REMAINING BUTTER. ONCE MELTED, POUR IT OVER THE PÂTÉ IN THE TERRINE OR SOUFFLÉ DISH. PRESS A PIECE OF PLASTIC WRAP DIRECTLY ONTO THE SURFACE OF THE PÂTÉ AND REFRIGERATE OVERNIGHT (12 OR MORE HOURS) OR UP TO 5 DAYS.

IN SMALL POT OVER MEDIUM HEAT, ADD THE CHERRIES, RED WINE VINEGAR, WATER, LEMON ZEST, AND SUGAR, AND BRING TO A SIMMER. REDUCE HEAT TO LOW, CONTINUE SIMMERING FOR ABOUT 5 MINUTES, THEN SET ASIDE.

SERVE THE PÂTÉ AT ROOM TEMPERATURE IN THE DISH ON A PLATTER, WITH THE MELBA TOAST AROUND IT, AND THE SWEET AND SOUR CHERRIES IN A BOWL ON THE SIDE.

Chicken Paillard

MAKES 4 SERVINGS

If you're looking for a quick and classic chicken dish that's good any time of year, this is it. The French paillard technique of butterflying meat, whether it's steak, chicken, or anything else, is a wonderful way to quickly and evenly cook animal proteins. I use it a lot in the kitchen. In terms of lightly pounding the chicken here, any sort of flat butcher mallet or reversible meat tenderizer works great. If you don't have either, well, the bottom of a pot works in a pinch.

4 skinless, boneless chicken breasts, butterflied and lightly pounded to about 1/4-inch thick
Kosher salt and freshly ground black pepper
4 tablespoons grapeseed oil (or other neutral oil), divided
1 teaspoon Dijon mustard
1 tablespoon red wine vinegar
3 tablespoons extra-virgin olive oil
2 cups loosely packed stemmed arugula
2 tablespoons roughly chopped roasted hazelnuts
Parmesan shavings, for garnish
4 lemon wedges, for garnish

Season the chicken breasts with salt and pepper. In a large cast-iron pan over medium heat, add 1 tablespoon of the oil. Once hot, carefully put one chicken breast into the pan and cook for 2 to 3 minutes, until golden brown. Flip and cook for another 2 to 3 minutes, or until cooked through. Transfer the chicken to a parchment paper-lined baking sheet. Repeat with the remaining chicken, adding 1 tablespoon of oil to the pan for each breast.

In a small jar, combine the mustard, vinegar, and olive oil. Top with a lid and shake vigorously until fully combined. In a medium bowl, lightly toss the arugula and hazelnuts with the dressing.

Serve each chicken breast with an equal amount of arugula salad, garnished with shaved Parmesan, and a lemon wedge.

THERE ARE MORE CHICKENS LIVING ON EARTH THAN PEOPLE!
OVER 3 BILLION IN CHINA ALONE.

MOST EGGS ARE LAID BETWEEN 7 A.M. AND 11 A.M.

A CHEF'S HAT IS SAID TO HAVE A
PLEAT FOR EACH OF THE MANY
WAYS YOU CAN COOK EGGS.

C

No MATTER THE YOLK COLOR, ALL EGGS ARE AN EXCELLENT SOURCE OF 8 ESSENTIAL NUTRIENTS, INCLUDING HIGH-QUALITY PROTEIN AND SEVERAL VITAMINS AND MINERALS; HOWEVER, YOLK COLOR CAN INDICATE THE PRESENCE OF ONE TYPE OF NUTRIENT — CAROTENOIDS. BEYOND CAROTENOIDS, YOLK COLOR DOES NOT INDICATE A MORE OR LESS NUTRITIOUS EGG.

C

MOST PEOPLE OF THE WORLD EAT THE EGG OF THE CHICKEN, GALLUS DOMESTICAS.

NEARLY 200 BREEDS AND VARIETIES OF CHICKENS HAVE BEEN ESTABLISHED WORLDWIDE.

MOST LAYING HENS IN THE U.S. ARE SINGLE-COMB WHITE LEGHORNS.

C

ChickenPM

Scottish Chicken Pie
Hainanese Chicken Rice
Doritos-Crusted Chicken Fingers & Crispy Potatoes
Indian Butter Chicken & Roti
Tandoori Chicken & Minty Yogurt Sauce
Mediterranean Chicken Sous Vide
Beer-Can Chicken Feast

Scottish Chicken Pie

MAKES 4 SERVINGS

This is a spin-off of the Scottish steak and kidney pie I grew up eating. I love savory pastry so much, and lobster pot pie is another personal favorite. This is an excellent winter dish for when it's really cold and snowing out, or there is a stretch of several days of heavy rain. It's another dependable comfort dish.

CRUST

1 1/4 cups all-purpose flour
1 teaspoon sugar
Pinch kosher salt
1 stick unsalted butter, cubed
4 tablespoons ice water
2 egg yolks, beaten

FILLING

2 skinless, boneless chicken breasts
2 tablespoons grapeseed oil (or other neutral oil), divided
Kosher salt and freshly ground black pepper
4 tablespoons unsalted butter
1/4 cup all-purpose flour
3 cups Chicken Stock (see page 10C), or good quality store-bought chicken broth
1 medium yellow onion, chopped
1 cup peeled and chopped carrots
1 cup chopped celery
1 cup fresh or frozen peas
1 cup sliced mushrooms
1 teaspoon minced fresh thyme leaves
1 tablespoon chopped fresh curly or flat-leaf parsley

Preheat the oven to 375 degrees F.
In the bowl of a food processor, combine the flour, sugar, and salt. Add the butter, breaking apart the cubes, and pulse until the mixture is slightly coarse. Add the ice water and pulse until the dough is crumbly. Transfer the dough to your work surface, shape it into a roughly 1-inch-thick disk, wrap it in plastic wrap, and refrigerate for at least 1 hour.

Line a baking sheet with foil, place the chicken breasts on it, brush 1 tablespoon of oil evenly all over them, and season with salt and pepper. Roast for 20 minutes, or until the internal temperature reaches 165 degrees F. Set aside to rest for about 10 minutes, and then slice it into 1/2-inch cubes.

In a medium pot over medium heat, melt the butter. Once melted, add the flour, stirring constantly for 1 to 2 minutes, until the roux begins to bubble and no longer smells like flour. Add the chicken stock, continue stirring and breaking up any bits of roux, and bring to a boil. Once boiling, season with salt and pepper, and set aside.

In a large pan over medium heat, add the remaining 1 tablespoon of oil. Once hot, add the onions, and carrots, and cook for 10 to 12 minutes, until the onions are translucent. Add the celery, peas, mushrooms, thyme, and parsley, and sauté for about 2 minutes. Add the cooked vegetables and cubed chicken to the chicken stock sauce, and stir to combine. Divide the filling evenly between 4 (roughly 2-cup) ovenproof dishes.

On a lightly floured surface, with a floured rolling pin, roll the dough out to an 1/8-inch thick rounded rectangle. Slice the dough into pieces that will cover the 4 ovenproof dishes, and then drape it over them. Trim and discard any overhanging dough. Brush the pie tops with the 2 beaten egg yolks. Place the pies on a baking sheet and bake for about 45 minutes, until the filling is bubbling and the pastry is golden brown. Set aside and let rest for about 10 minutes before serving.

EGG+CHICKEN

Hainanese Chicken Rice

MAKES 4 SERVINGS

You get a beautiful and complete meal with this national Singapore chicken dish. It's another deeply comforting jet lag or you-stayed-out-too-late dish, much like my Chicken Congee & Chinese Doughnut Sticks (see page 8c). I really like how when you poach chicken, as I have you do here, it ends up so soft and moist. Make this for a loved one when they're feeling bit under the weather and they'll be so grateful.

CHICKEN

2 (2 1/2 to 3 pound) whole chickens, trimmed of excess fat
Kosher salt
2 bunches of scallions, divided
1/4 cup sliced fresh ginger, divided
1 head garlic, sliced in half, divided
2 tablespoons toasted sesame oil, divided

RICE

2 tablespoons reserved chicken fat, chopped, or 2 tablespoons grapeseed oil (or other neutral oil)
3 tablespoons toasted sesame oil
1 tablespoon minced fresh ginger
1 tablespoon minced garlic
2 cups jasmine rice, rinsed
2 cups reserved chicken poaching water

CHILI SAUCE

5 Fresno chili peppers, stems and seeds removed, roughly chopped
2 garlic cloves
Juice of 1 lemon
2 tablespoons grapeseed oil (or other neutral oil)
1 teaspoon sugar
Kosher salt

GARNISH

1 to 2 tablespoons toasted white sesame seeds
1/4 cup pureed fresh ginger
1/4 cup soy sauce

Rinse the chickens and pat dry. Season them with salt, and stuff each cavity with one bunch of scallions, half of the ginger, and half of the garlic. Place the chickens in a stock pot filled with cold water. Bring to a boil and simmer for 25 to 30 minutes, or until the internal temperature of each chicken is 165 degrees F. Use tongs to transfer the chickens onto a wire rack over a rimmed baking sheet or roasting pan. Pat them dry and rub 1 tablespoon of sesame oil on each. Reserve the chicken poaching water for later use.

In a small pan over medium heat, render the chicken fat or melt the grapeseed oil for the rice. Add the sesame oil, ginger, and garlic, and sauté for 1 to 2 minutes until fragrant. Transfer the mixture to a rice cooker. Add the rice, 2 cups of the reserved poaching water, and set to cook. Alternately, cook the rice in a medium covered pot for 16 to 18 minutes, or until fully cooked.

In the bowl of a blender or food processor add the sauce's chilies, garlic, lemon juice, oil, sugar, and salt. If you have a variable speed blender, begin blending on low then raise the speed incrementally to liquify. Once fully blended, strain the sauce through a fine-mesh sieve into a small serving dish.

In a medium pot, add the 1 quart of the reserved chicken poaching water, and bring it to just about boiling and remove from heat.

Meanwhile, carve the chickens. Serve the chicken pieces family-style on a platter, with or without skin based on preference. Fluff the rice and serve it in small bowls, individually portioned, each sprinkled with sesame seeds. Ladle the hot chicken poaching water into small bowls, individually portioned, about 1 cup each. Serve the chili sauce, ginger puree, and soy sauce to pass at the table.

Doritos-Crusted Chicken Fingers & Crispy Potatoes

MAKES 4 TO 6 SERVINGS

I MADE THESE FOR MY SONS ALL THE TIME WHEN THEY WERE A BIT YOUNGER -- ALL DIFFERENT VARIATIONS OF THEM. THEY LOVE CHICKEN FINGERS. MOST KIDS DO. I THINK IT'S PRIMARILY BECAUSE THEY'RE SIMPLE, EASY TO EAT AND VERY FAMILIAR. THAT LAST BIT PLAYS A BIG PART. THE DORITOS HERE MAKE THE CHICKEN FINGERS CRISPY AND A LITTLE SPICY. THEY ALSO GIVE THEM A NICE, FUN COLOR.

---

4 CUPS GRAPESEED OIL (OR OTHER NEUTRAL OIL)
4 SKINLESS, BONELESS CHICKEN BREASTS
1 1/2 CUPS ALL-PURPOSE FLOUR
2 LARGE EGGS
4 CUPS DORITOS, PULSED IN FOOD PROCESSOR
1 1/2 CUPS BREAD CRUMBS
2 MEDIUM RUSSET POTATOES, PEELED AND SLICED INTO 1/2-INCH BATONS
KOSHER SALT
RANCH DRESSING, FOR SERVING

PREHEAT A DEEP FRYER OR LARGE HEAVY-BOTTOMED POT FILLED WITH THE GRAPESEED OIL TO 375 DEGREES F.

CUT EACH CHICKEN BREAST INTO LONG, 1-INCH-THICK STRIPS. ON A LARGE PLATE, ADD THE FLOUR. IN A MEDIUM SHALLOW BOWL, BEAT THE EGGS. ON ANOTHER LARGE PLATE, COMBINE THE DORITOS AND BREAD CRUMBS.

DREDGE EACH CHICKEN STRIP IN THE FLOUR, SHAKING OFF THE EXCESS. DIP THEM IN THE BEATEN EGG, LETTING ANY EXCESS DRIP OFF. COAT THEM IN THE DORITO-BREAD CRUMB MIX.

FRY THE ENCRUSTED CHICKEN IN SMALL BATCHES, 2 TO 3 PIECES OF CHICKEN AT A TIME, FOR 3 TO 4 MINUTES, UNTIL COOKED THROUGH, GOLDEN BROWN, AND CRISPY. USE A SLOTTED SPOON TO TRANSFER THEM TO A PAPER TOWEL-LINED BAKING SHEET.

PUT THE POTATOES INTO A LARGE BOWL FILLED WITH WATER.

LOWER THE DEEP FRYER OR HEAVY-BOTTOMED POT FILLED WITH GRAPESEED OIL TEMPERATURE TO 300 DEGREES F. PAT DRY THE POTATOES AND CAREFULLY DROP THEM INTO THE HOT OIL TO COOK FOR 5 MINUTES. TRANSFER TO A PAPER TOWEL-LINED BAKING SHEET. INCREASE THE TEMPERATURE OF THE OIL TO 350 DEGREES F, THEN FRY THE POTATOES AGAIN, IN 2 TO 3 BATCHES, FOR ABOUT 2 MINUTES, UNTIL GOLDEN AND COOKED THROUGH. TRANSFER TO A PAPER TOWEL-LINED BAKING SHEET AND SEASON WITH SALT.

SERVE EACH PERSON 3 TO 4 CHICKEN FINGERS, WITH A SIDE OF RANCH, AND A HANDFUL OF FRIES.

Indian Butter Chicken & Roti

MAKES 4 TO 6 SERVINGS

THE FIRST TIME I HAD INDIAN BUTTER CHICKEN I WAS IN TORONTO, BUT I ATE IT MOST FREQUENTLY WHEN I WAS IN SINGAPORE. THEIR LITTLE INDIA IS JUST EAST OF THE SINGAPORE RIVER. I FELL IN LOVE WITH BUTTER CHICKEN WHILE THERE, ON MY DAYS OFF AT VARIOUS FAMILY-RUN RESTAURANTS AROUND THE NEIGHBORHOOD. I ORDERED IT MOST OFTEN WITH FRESH BAKED, LIGHTLY CHARRED NAAN AND ICE-COLD TIGER BEER. SUCH A GOOD COMBO. YOU CAN COOK UP SOME BASMATI RICE AND A DAL FOR THIS, AS WELL, BUT YOU REALLY DON'T NEED TO. WHAT YOU DO NEED, HOWEVER, IS A COLD BEVERAGE.

1/4 CUP PLUS 2 TABLESPOONS EXTRA-VIRGIN OLIVE OIL

5 CLOVES GARLIC

2 FRESH FRESNO CHILIES, STEMMED AND SEEDED

2 MEDIUM YELLOW ONIONS, ROUGHLY CHOPPED

3 (1-INCH) PIECES PEELED FRESH GINGER

1/2 CUP GHEE

3 TABLESPOONS TOMATO PASTE

3 TABLESPOONS GROUND TURMERIC

2 TABLESPOONS CHILI POWDER

2 TABLESPOONS GARAM MASALA

2 TABLESPOONS GROUND CORIANDER

2 TABLESPOONS GROUND CUMIN

1 1/2 CUPS WATER

3 1/2 CUPS TOMATO PUREE

1 TEASPOON GROUND FENUGREEK LEAVES

4 SKINLESS, BONELESS CHICKEN LEGS

4 SKINLESS, BONELESS CHICKEN THIGHS

2 CUPS HEAVY CREAM

8 TABLESPOONS UNSALTED BUTTER

2 TEASPOONS STEMMED AND CHOPPED FRESH CILANTRO

KOSHER SALT AND FRESHLY GROUND BLACK PEPPER

4 PIECES STORE-BOUGHT ROTI OR NAAN, FOR SERVING

IN THE BOWL OF A BLENDER, COMBINE THE OLIVE OIL, GARLIC, CHILIES, ONION, AND GINGER, AND PUREE UNTIL SMOOTH.

IN A LARGE HEAVY-BOTTOMED POT OR DUTCH OVEN OVER MEDIUM-HIGH HEAT, HEAT THE GHEE. ONCE HOT, ADD THE ONION-CHILI PUREE AND COOK FOR 20 MINUTES, STIRRING OCCASIONALLY, UNTIL THE MIXTURE SLIGHTLY DARKENS AND SOFTENS. ADD THE TOMATO PASTE, TURMERIC, CHILI POWDER, GARAM MASALA, CORIANDER, AND CUMIN, AND COOK FOR ABOUT 5 MINUTES, UNTIL THE SAUCE IS DARK AND STICKY. ADD 1 1/2 CUPS OF WATER AND USE A WOODEN SPOON TO SCRAPE UP ANY BROWNED BITS AT THE BOTTOM OF THE PAN.

ADD THE TOMATO PUREE AND FENUGREEK, INCREASE THE HEAT TO HIGH, AND BRING TO A BOIL. LOWER THE HEAT, COVER, AND MAINTAIN A SIMMER, STIRRING OCCASIONALLY, FOR ABOUT 1 HOUR, UNTIL THE SAUCE HAS THICKENED. ADD THE CHICKEN AND COOK UNTIL IT IS COOKED THROUGH, ABOUT 15 MINUTES. ADD THE CREAM, BUTTER, AND CILANTRO, AND STIR TO COMBINE. SEASON WITH SALT AND PEPPER TO TASTE.

IN A MEDIUM NONSTICK PAN OVER HIGH HEAT, TOAST THE ROTI OR NAAN ON EACH SIDE FOR ABOUT 30 SECONDS UNTIL SLIGHTLY CRISP.

SLICE THE ROTI OR NAAN INTO TRIANGLES AND SERVE ALONGSIDE THE BUTTER CHICKEN IN BOWLS.

Tandoori Chicken & Minty Yogurt Sauce

MAKES 4 SERVINGS

Tandoori chicken is the perfect meal for a Sunday afternoon with a 6-pack of beer . I love it. I ate it the most when I lived in Singapore for several years. There's a sizeable Indian population there and the Indian food culture is impressive. If you ever get the chance to eat tandoori chicken from an actual Indian tandoor, (a cylindrical coal oven used for cooking and baking) please don't pass it up. Those big tandoor drums, with wildly hot coals at the bottom, emit the most incredible smells. They often get up to 900 degrees! Don't worry, your oven doesn't need to get that hot to prepare my tandoori chicken at home.

---

2 cups plain whole milk yogurt, divided
1 medium sweet onion, diced
1 garlic clove, minced
1/2 teaspoon ground ginger
1 teaspoon ground coriander
1/2 teaspoon chili powder
1/2 teaspoon ground cumin
1 teaspoon garam masala
1 tablespoon white wine vinegar, divided
1 tablespoon Worcestershire sauce
Juice of 1 lemon
Kosher salt and freshly ground black pepper
4 bone-in, skin-on chicken breasts
2 tablespoons stemmed and chopped fresh mint
1 loaf of crusty bread of your choice, sliced and toasted
8 lime wedges

In a large bowl, combine 1 cup of the yogurt, with the onion, garlic, ginger, coriander, chili powder, cumin, garam masala, 1 teaspoon of the vinegar, Worcestershire sauce, lemon juice, salt, and pepper. Stir well to blend. Cut 3 to 4 slices (roughly 1/2-inch-deep) across each chicken breast. In a dish deep enough to hold the chicken, pour the yogurt mixture over the chicken breasts, turning the pieces to coat them on all sides. Cover and refrigerate overnight (12 or more hours).

Preheat the oven to 375 degrees F.

Remove the chicken from the marinade, scraping off any excess. Set the chicken on a foil-lined baking sheet and roast for 20 to 25 minutes, or until the internal temperature reaches 165 degrees F. Set aside and let rest for about 10 minutes.

In a small bowl, stir together the remaining yogurt, along with the mint, and remaining 2 teaspoons of vinegar.

To serve, place the chicken alongside dollops of mint yogurt, with toasted bread, and lime wedges.

Sous Vide Mediterranean Chicken & Tomato Basil Salad

MAKES 4 SERVINGS

Sous vide is a wonderful technique that I highly recommend trying if you haven't. That said, I've included steps below for how to make this dish without a home sous vide set-up. One of the biggest benefits of sous vide is perfectly cooked, juicy and tender proteins, that are really quick and easy to finish off before serving. You can use any heirloom tomatoes for the salad here, but I always love the pear-shaped ones if you can find them. They're delicious and present really well.

Juice of 2 lemons, divided
1/2 cup extra-virgin olive oil, divided
6 sprigs fresh thyme, divided
2 sprigs fresh rosemary, divided
8 garlic cloves, divided
1 (2 1/2 to 3 pound) whole chicken, halved
Kosher salt and freshly ground black pepper
2 pints small heirloom tomatoes, quartered
3 tablespoons fresh chopped basil
1/4 cup diced red onion
1 tablespoon red wine vinegar

In a large pot filled with water to three-quarters-full, preheat your sous vide cooker to 150 degrees F. Prepare two, gallon-size Ziploc bags. In each bag, add half of the lemon juice, 2 tablespoons of olive oil, 3 sprigs of thyme, 1 sprig of rosemary, and 3 smashed garlic cloves. Season the halved chicken with salt and pepper then place one half in each bag. Seal the bags removing as much air as possible, by pressing down on the bag and contents. Place the bags in the water bath and cook for 6 hours.

Once the chicken has finished cooking, transfer each half from its bag to a baking sheet and set aside.

Meanwhile, in a large cast-iron skillet over high heat, add 1 tablespoon of the olive oil. Once smoking, press one of the chicken halves into the pan skin-side down for about 2 minutes. Flip and cook for another 2 minutes. Repeat with the remaining chicken half and an additional 1 tablespoon of olive oil.

In a medium bowl, combine the tomatoes, basil, and red onion. Mince the remaining 2 garlic cloves. In a small bowl, whisk together the remaining 2 tablespoons of olive oil, along with the red wine vinegar, minced garlic, and salt and pepper to taste. Toss the tomato mix with the dressing.

Serve the chicken on a large platter with the tomato basil salad spooned over the top.

If you do not have a home sous vide set-up, don't worry. You can still make this recipe. Simply fill the large pot to three-quarters-full as in the recipe, and place it over medium-low heat. Mount a thermometer on the side of the pot, so that it is submerged in the water. Follow the steps above in terms of filling the Ziploc bags. Once the water reaches 150 degrees F, hang the Ziploc chicken bags in the water with the tops of the bags open, so that air can escape, and clip them in place with a binder clip or kitchen clip. Bring the water back to 150 degrees F, and once it is there, set your timer for 6 hours. Monitor the pot and increase or decrease the heat (adding water if necessary to keep the chicken submerged) to keep the water as close to 150 degrees F as possible, for the entire cook time. After the 6-hour cook time, carry on with the recipe above by searing the chicken and preparing the salad.

EGG+CHICKEN

Beer-Can Chicken Feast

MAKES 6 TO 8 SERVINGS

I FIRST PUT THIS ON THE MENU AT NEW REALM BREWING CO. IN ATLANTA, GEORGIA FIVE OR SIX YEARS AGO. IT'S A REALLY FUN MENU ITEM AND PEOPLE LOVE IT. THE RESTAURANT IS TOO BIG AND CROWDED, WITH ITS 700 SEATS, TO ACTUALLY SERVE THE CHICKEN ON THE BEER CANS IN THE DINING ROOM, BUT THE FLAVOR AND JUICINESS FROM COOKING IT THAT WAY IS ALL THERE. THE IPA PERMEATES THE WHOLE BIRD. THE MAIN THING THAT CAN GO WRONG WITH THIS DISH IS OVERCOOKING THE CHICKEN, SO CHECK ON IT HERE AND THERE, AND HAVE YOUR THERMOMETER AT THE READY. ALSO, BE SURE TO LET THE BIRDS COOL DOWN A BIT BEFORE YOU PUT YOUR STURDY KITCHEN GLOVES AND CAREFULLY PULL THEM OFF OF THE CANS.

BRINE
1 CUP KOSHER SALT
1/4 CUP SUGAR
2 CUPS HOT WATER
5 1/2 CUPS (ABOUT 4 CANS) IPA BEER
1 LEMON, SLICED
1 ORANGE, SLICED
8 FRESH SAGE LEAVES
2 SPRIGS FRESH ROSEMARY
1 SPRIG FRESH THYME
1 TABLESPOON FENNEL SEED, TOASTED
1 TABLESPOON CORIANDER SEED, TOASTED
1 TABLESPOON BLACK PEPPERCORNS, TOASTED
2 GARLIC CLOVES, SMASHED
1 SHALLOT, PEELED AND QUARTERED
2 (2 1/2 TO 3 POUND) WHOLE CHICKENS, TRIMMED OF EXCESS FAT

DRY RUB
1 TEASPOON GARLIC POWDER
1 TEASPOON ONION POWDER
2 TABLESPOONS SUGAR
1 TABLESPOON PLUS 1 TEASPOON GROUND PAPRIKA
1 TABLESPOON PLUS 1 TEASPOON CHILI POWDER
2 TEASPOONS FINELY GROUND WHITE PEPPER
1 TEASPOON KOSHER SALT
1 TEASPOON GROUND MUSTARD

CHICKEN & PAN SAUCE
2 (12-OUNCE) CANS OF IPA BEER
1/2 CUP PEELED AND CHOPPED CARROTS
1/2 CUP CHOPPED WHITE ONION
1/2 CUP CHOPPED CELERY
1/4 CUP WHITE WINE
1 CUP CHICKEN STOCK (SEE PAGE 10C) OR GOOD-QUALITY STORE-BOUGHT CHICKEN BROTH
1 TEASPOON TOMATO PASTE
1 TABLESPOON UNSALTED BUTTER

MASHED POTATOES
3 1/2 POUNDS YUKON GOLD POTATOES (ABOUT 6 LARGE)
1 CUP WHOLE MILK
1/2 STICK UNSALTED BUTTER, CUBED
KOSHER SALT AND FINELY GROUND WHITE PEPPER

BRAISED BABY CARROTS
1 POUND RAINBOW BABY CARROTS
1 TABLESPOON GRAPESEED OIL
2 TABLESPOONS UNSALTED BUTTER
1 TEASPOON CHOPPED FRESH THYME LEAVES
KOSHER SALT AND FRESHLY GROUND BLACK PEPPER

Beer-Can Chicken Feast

DAY ONE

In a container or pot large enough to submerge both chickens, stir the salt and sugar into the water until dissolved. Add the 5 and 1/2 cups of IPA, lemon, orange, sage, rosemary, thyme, fennel, coriander, black peppercorns, garlic, and shallot, and stir to combine. Submerge both chickens in the brine. Cover and refrigerate for 24 hours.

DAY TWO

Preheat the oven to 375 degrees F.
In a small bowl, mix together the garlic powder, onion powder, sugar, paprika, chili powder, white pepper, salt, and ground mustard.
Remove the chickens from the brine and pat them dry. On a baking sheet, rub the dry rub all over the chickens.

Stand the opened beer cans on a roasting pan. Holding each chicken upright, lower it over a can so that the can goes into the main cavity. Pull the chicken legs forward so that the chickens sit upright. Add the chopped carrots, onion, and celery around the pan. Carefully transfer the chickens to the oven, and roast for 50 to 60 minutes, or until the skin is golden brown and crisp, and the internal temperature in the thickest part of the thighs of each chicken reaches 165 degrees F.
Set aside and let rest for 10 to 15 minutes. Carefully remove the cans, carve the chickens, and arrange the pieces on a platter. Discard the vegetables, and set aside the roasting pan and its juices for the sauce.

In a large pot over high heat, cover the potatoes in water, and bring to a boil. Reduce the heat to medium-low, and lightly boil for 35 to 40 minutes, or until fork tender. Meanwhile, in a small pot over medium heat, bring the milk to a light boil. Reduce the heat to low to keep the milk warm.
Use a slotted spoon to transfer the potatoes to a large plate or platter, and cool until warm. While still warm, remove and discard the skins, and transfer the potatoes to a potato ricer. Pass them through the ricer into a medium pot, and then put the pot over medium heat. Whisk the potatoes while adding half of the warm milk, stirring to combine. Add the cubed butter. If the potatoes are too dry, slowly add more milk until they reach the desired texture. Season with salt and white pepper.

Over high heat, bring a medium pot of water to a boil. Add the rainbow carrots to the pot and boil for about 10 minutes. Use a slotted spoon to transfer the carrots to a paper towel-lined plate. In a large pan over high heat, add the oil. Once hot, add the carrots and toss to coat with oil. Add the butter and thyme, and toss to evenly coat. Cook for another 1 to 2 minutes, and season with salt and pepper.
Set the roasting pan with the reserved juices over high heat and cook for 1 to 2 minutes. Deglaze the pan by adding the white wine and chicken stock, scraping up any browned bits. Stir in the tomato paste until incorporated, and simmer for 1 to 2 minutes. Strain the pan sauce through a fine-mesh sieve into a medium pan. Set the pan over high heat and bring to a boil. Reduce the heat to low, and simmer for 12 to 15 minutes, or until the pan sauce has slightly thickened. Stir in the butter.
Serve the carved chicken, mashed potatoes, pan sauce, and baby carrots family-style.

Lemon Oil

Finishes 25 Dishes

Something I am very fond of for finishing and giving a pop to a lot of our dishes in the book. The right amount of acid to help you digest nicely any dish. The shelf life is 2-3 months.

---

6 LEMONS
4 STICKS FROM THE BOTTOM OF LEMONGRASS CRUSHED
1/2 CUP GRAPESEED OIL
1/2 CUP HAZELNUT OIL
PINCH OF SALT

Peel the lemon rind into long, wide strips, and place them in a medium bowl. Add the lemongrass, grapeseed oil, hazelnut oil, and pinch of salt to the bowl. Cover and infuse at room temperature for 48 hours. Strain the oil through a fine-mesh sieve, discarding the lemon peels and lemongrass, and store in a lidded jar at room temperature for up to 3 months.

WHILE THERE IS SOME EVIDENCE OF NATIVE FOWL IN THE AMERICAS PRIOR TO COLUMBUS' ARRIVAL, IT IS BELIEVED THAT ON HIS SECOND TRIP IN 1493, COLUMBUS CARRIED THE FIRST CHICKENS TO THE NEW WORLD.

EGGS WERE COLORED, BLESSED, EXCHANGED AND EATEN AS PART OF THE RITES OF SPRING LONG BEFORE CHRISTIAN TIMES.

EGGS ARE ONE OF THE MOST CONCENTRATED FOOD SOURCES OF CHOLINE, A NUTRIENT ESSENTIAL FOR NORMAL FUNCTIONING OF ALL CELLS, BUT PARTICULARLY IMPORTANT DURING PREGNANCY TO SUPPORT HEALTHY BRAIN DEVELOPMENT OF THE FETUS.

THE NUTRIENTS FOUND IN EGGS CAN PLAY A ROLE IN WEIGHT MANAGEMENT, MUSCLE STRENGTH, HEALTHY PREGNANCY, BRAIN FUNCTION, EYE HEALTH AND MORE.

EGGS CONTAIN LUTEIN AND ZEAXANTHIN, ANTIOXIDANTS THAT ARE BELIEVED TO REDUCE THE RISK OF DEVELOPING CATARACTS AND SLOW THE PROGRESSION OF AGE-RELATED MACULAR DEGENERATION, A DISEASE THAT DEVELOPS WITH AGE.

A *Richard Grant in the Kitchen*

SMALL PASTRY OF DRIED EGG FOAM AND SUGAR FROM WHICH THE SIMPLIFIED MERINGUE EVOLVED. ITS FAME SPREAD AND MARIE ANTOINETTE IS SAID TO HAVE PREPARED THE SWEET WITH HER OWN HANDS AT THE TRIANON IN FRANCE.

SPEAKING OF FRANCE, IT WAS AN EGG...A SOFT-BOILED EGG OR OEUFS MOLLETS... THAT STUMPED THE FAMOUS CHEF JULIA CHILD DURING HER FINAL EXAM.

IF AN EGG IS ACCIDENTALLY DROPPED ON THE FLOOR, SPRINKLE IT HEAVILY WITH SALT FOR EASY CLEAN UP.

MORE ABOUT CAROTENOIDS AND YOLK COLOR:
CAROTENOIDS ARE RESPONSIBLE FOR THE PIGMENT OF NOT ONLY EGG YOLKS, BUT ALSO COLORFUL FRUITS AND VEGETABLES. MOST EGG YOLKS IN THE U.S. ARE BRIGHT YELLOW OR YELLOW-ORANGE DUE TO THE CAROTENOIDS LUTEIN AND ZEAXANTHIN USUALLY FROM THE CORN IN THE HEN'S DIET.

IN SOME CASES, MARIGOLD PETALS OR RED PEPPERS ARE ADDED TO A HEN'S FEED, WHICH CAN CHANGE THE CAROTENOID CONTENT AND THE PIGMENT OF THE YOLK TO A MORE ORANGE/GOLD COLOR.

Double-yolked eggs (or "double yolkers") are usually produced by young hens whose egg production cycles are not yet completely synchronized.

Book Production Team -Alesandro, Ray, Bill, Grant and Sam

MORE THAN 96 BILLION TABLE EGGS ARE PRODUCED IN THE U.S. ANNUALLY.
MOST OF THEM ARE SOLD AT THE STORE, EATEN AT RESTAURANTS OR GO INTO OTHER FOODS AS AN INGREDIENT.
SOME GO INTO PET FOOD OR EVEN FERTILIZER.
BUT NONE OF THESE EGGS IS WASTED.

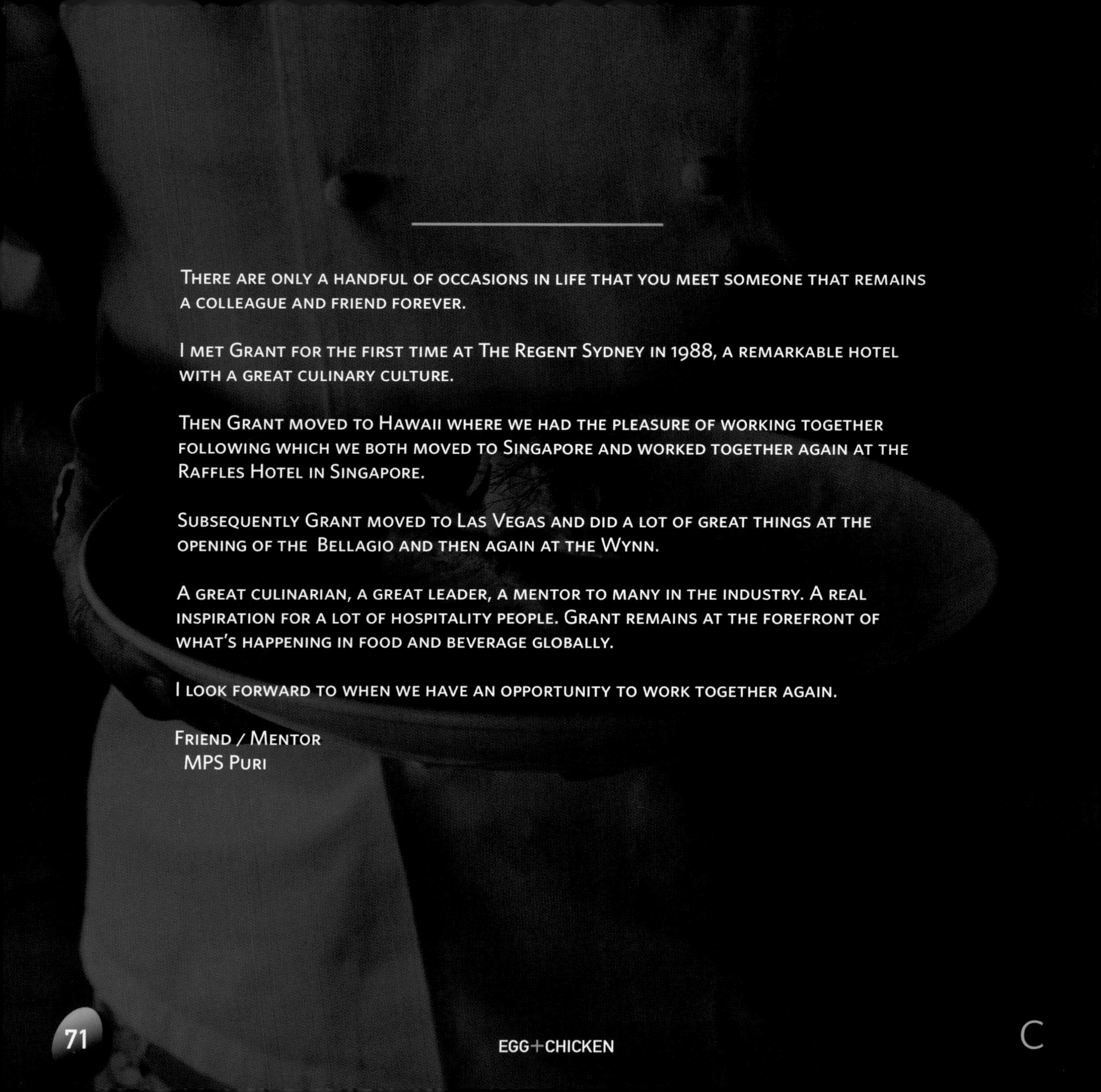

There are only a handful of occasions in life that you meet someone that remains a colleague and friend forever.

I met Grant for the first time at The Regent Sydney in 1988, a remarkable hotel with a great culinary culture.

Then Grant moved to Hawaii where we had the pleasure of working together following which we both moved to Singapore and worked together again at the Raffles Hotel in Singapore.

Subsequently Grant moved to Las Vegas and did a lot of great things at the opening of the Bellagio and then again at the Wynn.

A great culinarian, a great leader, a mentor to many in the industry. A real inspiration for a lot of hospitality people. Grant remains at the forefront of what's happening in food and beverage globally.

I look forward to when we have an opportunity to work together again.

Friend / Mentor
MPS Puri

C

CHICKEN